Reclaiming Motherhood

Reclaiming Motherhood

from a Culture Gone Mad

Samantha N. Stephenson

Our Sunday Visitor
Huntington, Indiana

Nihil Obstat
Msgr. Michael Heintz, Ph.D.
Censor Librorum

Imprimatur
✠ Kevin C. Rhoades
Bishop of Fort Wayne-South Bend
June 27, 2022

The *Nihil Obstat* and *Imprimatur* are official declarations that a book is free from doctrinal or moral error. It is not implied that those who have granted the *Nihil Obstat* and *Imprimatur* agree with the contents, opinions, or statements expressed.

Our Sunday Visitor Publishing Division
Our Sunday Visitor, Inc., 200 Noll Plaza, Huntington, IN 46750; www.osv.com;
1-800-348-2440

ISBN: 978-1-68192-775-6 (Inventory No. T2646)
RELIGION—Christian Theology—Ethics.
RELIGION—Christian Living—Women's Interests.
RELIGION—Christianity—Catholic.
eISBN: 978-1-68192-776-3
LCCN: 2022944122

Cover and interior design: Lindsey Riesen
Cover art: Adobe Stock

PRINTED IN THE UNITED STATES OF AMERICA

For Garrett, my great love,

*and for Charlotte, Bennett, Noah, and
Chiara, my shooting stars*

Contents

Introduction

*We are at a crossroads. Today the mission of women is
to become conscious of the beauty and dignity of their
function. And by so doing, they will reconquer men
[for God]. ... Until women rediscover the beauty of their
mission and stand for life, the world is doomed.*

Alice von Hildebrand[1]

To become a parent is to become a steward of God's
precious gift of life. And yet we find ourselves in a
culture where, far from being treated with awe, the family
is being dissected. Motherhood, central to the identity of
women, is being erased from our minds, while the self-evident notion that men and women contribute uniquely
to the world becomes cultural heresy. Parenthood is less
often understood as a gift and is more often valued in

market terms. Women are treated as raw material for the production of children — who come with a price tag. The future of the unborn is increasingly predicated upon possession of characteristics that merit continued existence. Women are told that *all* that matters in the delivery room is a healthy baby, and that indeed, they are not "women" any longer but "birthing persons," "people who menstruate," or "bodies with vaginas." Does contraception prevent abortions, or does it paradoxically increase the need for them? What does the evidence say?

Our age is fraught with lies that, if left unexamined, seep into our thinking, slowly poisoning us against God's truth. These lies permeate secular culture but can also be recognized as motivating influences within our Church. If we are honest, we might even recognize them in our own minds. As if in a warped game of telephone, Enlightenment philosopher René Descartes's profound declaration, "I think, therefore I am," has devolved into the chant of postmodernity: "I am whatever I think I am." Our culture has bought into the lie that if the truth hurts, then it must be rejected in favor of some more palatable reality. When the truth hurts, we simply make up our own.

We have made each individual into his own god, one whose own will is paramount — provided it does not impinge upon the will of another — and whose only guide is his own experience of pleasure and fulfillment. This is a philosophy of selfishness and isolation under the guise of freedom. This stunted paradigm of personal growth sees freedom from constraint as a precondition for happiness.

Within this paradigm, children become objects: They are either obstacles to their mother's flourishing (defined narrowly in economic terms) or else trophies to be collected to satiate her desire for fulfillment through the status of motherhood.

Rediscovering Motherhood through Church Teaching and Sound Bioethics

There is an alternative narrative, one that frees women to become who they are — not through the piling up of accomplishments, but by the sacrifice of self. Our Church tells a powerful story about women and motherhood, about our place as bearers and nurturers of life. We blossom as the caretakers of our children and of one another as our acts of love generate more love and life within our world. The cultural experiments of the last sixty years have yielded a world starving for love and growing lonelier as family ties wane. We need a cultural revival on the issues of womanhood, motherhood, sexuality, and life. Only by living within a paradigm that honors the self-gift of motherhood as the pinnacle of womanhood can love, and not self-interest, begin once again to order our lives.

Our Church continues to stay the course amidst the madness. She still boldly proclaims the truth of our identity as creatures, sons and daughters of a Creator who imbues our lives with meaning. It is not for us to generate our own path to fulfillment, but to perceive and act on that truth which He has placed deep within our hearts: a yearning for relationship with Him and a drive to find our own identity in self-gift to one another. The truth the Church safeguards and proclaims is not opposed to our good; it is the path toward it. This is the truth we must absorb, live, and radiate to our culture, a culture that is utterly confused about what leads to real meaning and authentic joy.

This book is an attempt to explore the truth of who we are as mothers in the context of the lies we face in our present-day culture. In many ways, the contemporary attacks on our femininity and our fertility provide us with new ways of understanding and unpacking the Revelation that the Holy Spirit has imparted to the Church throughout the ages. Although this truth is steadfast and unchanging, our understanding of it develops throughout time as new social and scientific developments reveal different facets of God's unchanging plan for our lives. Learning to unpack this plan in light of our current cultural circumstances, to "read the signs of the times," is an essential aspect of our call as Christians, as articulated in *Gaudium et Spes*. The following chapters present, in light of God's Revelation, a cross-examination of current social and medical trends threatening to dismantle motherhood.

While rampant social attacks on motherhood and femininity might seem overwhelming, the Church is steeped in centuries of wisdom — consisting in both thought and lived witness — about the meaning and dignity of womanhood. We have a wealth of knowledge gleaned from the Revelation of Sacred Scripture, the lives of the saints, and the reflections of thinkers, such as St.

Edith Stein and St. John Paul II, who expounded on the feminine genius. Chapter 1 lays the foundation for the thinking in this book by reviewing some of the lies our culture promotes and holding them up against the truths proclaimed by the Church. Drawing on the wealth of the Church's wisdom, the chapters on the social crises of the attack on femininity (chapter 2), the disappearance of the family (chapter 3), and the working mom dilemma (chapter 8) argue that the enduring truth of God's message does not change with the times. Chapter 12 first argues that we have been socialized to believe the fallacy that speaking out on behalf of this truth equates to being "judgmental," and, second, empowers the reader to embrace our prophetic call to spiritual motherhood.

Readers who wish to dive directly into magisterial teaching on bioethical questions — the moral questions that arise within medical care, research, and technology — would do well to investigate the two most recent instructions on the topic from the Congregation for the Doctrine of the Faith, *Donum Vitae* (1987) and *Dignitas Personae* (2008). When *Donum Vitae* was released, the *Los Angeles Times* called it "an all-out attack" on scientific advancements.[2] Such a view represents one of the defining paradigms of our culture: scientism, which relies on the assumption that all technological advancements are good. Others hold that scientific progress is at best neutral, creating new tools whose morality is not intrinsic to their use but dependent upon the purposes of those who wield them. Think of dynamite or nuclear fission; these technologies carry with them the potential for both great good and great evil.

Reproductive technologies are different. They are tools that *in themselves* work to redefine basic concepts of our humanity, including motherhood and the family. These reproductive technologies transform the gift of life into an object of manipulation, thereby redefining the meaning of human existence. As such, the choice to employ them is never merely individual and cannot be value-neutral. The ends or desires of those who use these technologies cannot justify their use. *Donum Vitae* and *Dignitas Personae* argue that these technologies are intrinsically immoral. *Reclaiming Motherhood*'s chapters on prenatal testing (chapter 5), IVF (chapter 9), surrogacy (chapter 10), and emerging reproductive technologies (chapter 11) draw on the wisdom of these documents and elaborate on ways to uphold human dignity in these areas.

Chapters on contraception (chapter 4), childbirth (chapter 6), and nursing (chapter 7) examine Scripture and the saints to help us understand the meaning and mystery of who we as women are created to be while also highlighting the bioethical questions at stake. The design of our bodies is not happenstance, but intentional. Our fertility is not a pathology to be controlled, but a gift from our Creator to lead us more deeply to the truth of who we are created to be in love and relationship. From the doctor's office to the corporate office, from the pews to our own homes, this book unpacks cultural narratives and defends the truth of the Church, giving readers permission to say "no" to practices that violate human dignity and to say "yes" to the beauty of God's gifts of motherhood and the family.

A Mission of Love

This book places the moral teachings of the Church in the context of God's vision for our vocation and true happiness as mothers. Reclaiming motherhood means reclaiming our responsibility as stewards of the truth about who we are and how we are meant to live, and this book equips us to carry out that mission. As women, we have within our nature a unique capacity to embrace and proclaim the truth in love. Whether or not we have been granted the gift of physical motherhood, we are all called to spiritual motherhood: This calling impels us to communicate the truth to the people God has placed in our lives, who are in a very real sense our spiritual children. We do this not in the spirit of condemnation that our culture so fears, but in a spirit of love, because in a world starved for meaning we are fortunate to be in possession of the bread that truly satisfies.

Reclaiming motherhood encompasses more than ensuring that our reproductive practices are ethical. It means proclaiming the beauty of the marital covenant as the wellspring of love that gives rise to a family and nurtures our children. It means preserving the unique contributions of masculinity and femininity in shaping a child's identity. It means respecting the dignity of every woman and child, treating each individual as an end in himself and never merely the instrumental means to serve the will of another. It means keeping a firm grasp on those things that make us human. We must lift our voices to declare that social progress must never be measured in purely scientific terms. Instead, our progress as a society is reflected in how well we love one another and ensure that each member has the opportunity to experience full human flourishing.

It is on this point that the Church and our culture can still agree, and so this must be our point of departure: What is truly good for every member of our society should be the motivating force behind our moral decisions. Our society has been duped into thinking that this good lies in whatever each individual determines for himself. The reality is that we cannot flourish in such isolation. We were not made to. At the heart of every human person is not merely his own will but the capacity and longing for relationship. Real happiness lies not in doing whatever we would like, but in being what we were made to be. As we examine emerging medical practices and social reconstructions in the following pages, let us bear these truths in mind: What makes us more loving, invites us deeper into community, and shapes us most clearly in the image of our Creator? May the burning of these questions be the fire of the Holy Spirit blazing within us, enabling us to communicate the truth that resonates in every human heart.

It is not too late. Now is a critical moment for women to embrace the good fruits of the Women's Movement while rejecting those things that run contrary to our good and that threaten to further depersonalize us. It isn't too late, but the clock is ticking. More is at stake in reclaiming motherhood than personal medical decisions. We must critically examine these practices and reflect on their implications so that we can use our prophetic voices to protect future women and children from grave violations of their personhood. If we don't turn back the tide on these practices, we run the risk of being swept along by the currents of madness.

CHAPTER 1

The Spiritual Roots
of Our Madness

"You will be like God" (Gn 3:5). These words of the serpent to Eve, mother of all the living, echo in our hearts today. We live in a culture that feeds us a falsely empowering narrative: We can be whatever we wish to be. The world tells us to seek happiness in whatever way we define it, and that any road can lead to happiness if we believe it will. Our society faces depression and anxiety at skyrocketing levels, much of which can be traced back to this narrative: If we are not happy, it is up to us to find what will fill us. As our efforts fall short, we are left pursuing dream after dream until our failed attempts leave us despondent. We are unhappy, and it is our own failings that have made us that way. The pressure to fulfill oneself mounts; it is an anxiety we were not made to bear.

Why begin here? Why begin a discussion of motherhood with the failings of our first mother, the mother of all the living? Because, as St. Edith Stein says, we all have something of Eve in us, and it is up to us to find our way to Mary.[1] We have a brokenness that needs healing: a fundamental lack of trust that what God offers us is truly good. If we are to dismantle the misperceptions and flat-out lies our culture promotes, to rediscover the beauty of God's plan for our femininity, for motherhood, and for the family, then we must return to the central truth that God is God and we are not. If we can recover a sense of reverence for the giftedness of our existence, we can assume a posture of humility and seek to understand the wisdom in the way that God has made the world.

The Poisonous Lie We've Swallowed

Much of the struggle we have in understanding and embracing God's plan for marriage, fertility, and the family stems from this original conflict. A return to Eve reveals that the Father of Lies has no new tricks. We find the same lies eating away at us beneath the surface today as those that led our first parents astray. We reject the sovereignty of God and refuse to live according to our nature; we prefer to be gods ourselves. This fundamental refusal to be creatures permeates our thinking and cripples our will. Unpacking these lies allows us to let go of the fear and anxiety that keep us trapped in mistrust of the God who has given us everything.

The serpent's words to Eve form the central lie that leads us all not just to eternal death, but also to living as those who are dead already. We have inherited the original sin of our first parents, and we continue to feed on a diet that fails to satisfy and leaves us empty. We need the bread of life Himself: the way, the truth, and the life.

We have been designed for happiness. That is why our inmost being whispers to us that happiness does exist. That is why we go to such lengths to chase it. The problem is that God did not intend for us to design our own plan for happiness. We are not made for just any road or destination. We are made for heaven, and God has given us the gift of the Church's moral teachings as a GPS to guide us along the right route. There may be some wiggle room on whether we take the freeway or the scenic route, but there are definitely wrong routes that lead us far from where we wish to go, and there is only *one* destination that will satisfy us. It is when we fail to recognize this, when we decide to go it alone, that we find ourselves utterly lost.

Jesus is the way, the truth, and the life. He has promised us, "My yoke is easy and my burden is light" (Mt 11:30), and yet so many of us remain suspicious. We like to pick and choose those teachings by which we abide. Like our first parents, we accept what appeals to us about our faith and remain wary of all else. As G. K. Chesterton observed, "The Christian ideal has not been tried and found wanting; it has been found difficult, and left untried."[2]

Which is it? Is it easy, as Jesus promises, or difficult,

as Chesterton observed? Paradoxically, it is both. Once lived, the Christian way of life, a life of sanctity on the long road to holiness, is a road of joy. Whatever obstacles are encountered along the way, we surmount them with a lightness that buoys our journey because we are filled with the fuel we were made for: the fuel of love that ignites, combusts, and impels us along the way.

Our difficulty lies in the will. We prefer comfort to almost all else and would rather sit by the roadside, allowing the inertia of ease to keep us frozen there and never entering the real adventure of life. Or if we do enter that adventure, we choose to fill ourselves with the wrong kind of fuel. We let anger and vice isolate us and erode our connections so that we make our pilgrimage alone. We blind ourselves to the road we ought to take.

This lie that we will be like God is the poison that feeds so many other lies, all designed to keep us on the roadside, off route, or fueling up with what blinds and imprisons us. Each lie is a barrier; if we are willing to dismantle these lies, we can progress to sainthood with joy — unburdened, as Jesus describes it. Real freedom is not choosing anything at all, but rather choosing that which leads to the highest good. As mothers, we need to instill in our children a vision of our lives as opportunities to give ourselves in service and in love. When we understand our purpose as given, rather than self-generated, we can equip and empower our children to discover their purpose in relationship with Jesus.

Like Eve, we suffer from a fundamental mistrust of

God's promises to us; we refuse to be who God made us to be, always on the lookout for something better. Satan capitalizes on this weakness by whispering to us promises of his own. His path is seductive and his burden difficult to perceive — until we find ourselves crushed beneath that burden, unable to pave our own way out.

Mary, Our Champion and Model of Obedience

We have a champion. Far from being crushed by the burden of sin, Mary has crushed Satan beneath her heel (see Gn 3:15). In her humble trust and obedience, she makes up for what Eve lacks. As mothers, we must first embrace Mary's example and live in this obedience ourselves. Only then can we live (and equip our children to live) as witnesses of the joy-filled Christian life and radiate this joy to others through our spiritual motherhood.

Modeling ourselves after Mary is urgent in our "you do you" society — a society that denies the reality that our bodies are meant to signify, defines female empowerment as sexual promiscuity and the right to exterminate our children within us, and denigrates traditional cultural roles of women without asking what wisdom these roles might have held. Our societal view of "progress" is narrow, encouraging only those behaviors that knock down the walls of the past rather than attempting to glean wisdom by understanding why these walls were constructed. The fact is that we have much to learn about who we are and how we are meant to live from those who have gone before us, especially those whose lives honored the God who made them.

In forgetting Who is sovereign, society has taken the wrong road. We have followed Eve, seeing ourselves as merely first among the animals, putting our will above all else. What a tragedy, when we are made for so much more. Now more than ever, we need to cling to Mary's Fiat, recognizing that she crushes Satan's head not by force but by deference to the will of God. We need to learn to live by and embrace every teaching of our Holy Mother the Church, and to do so with joy. We may struggle greatly with this. But it is in our "yes" even in the midst of struggle, in our assent despite our reservations, that we are able to be fully receptive to the wonders God holds for us. When we say "yes" to our loving Father, our good King, and rightly acknowledge His authority, we surrender the power we have tried to grasp but ultimately are not made to wield. Can we trust God enough to let Him be God?

Our Twisted Cultural Narratives

We are in an age of the New Babel; while we may be able to communicate through our words, we have lost the ability to dialogue at a more fundamental level. The philosophies of our modern age have contributed to our understanding of the centrality of conscience and opened the door to increased ecumenical and interreligious dialogue. At the same time, though, detached from the grace and truth of Christ, these ways of thinking about the world become twisted. The purpose of this chapter is not to trace these intellectual developments but to provide an overview of the inheritance our culture has uncritically received from them — to name the lies we have come to accept, to reiterate truth in its untwisted form, and, in so doing, to shore up our moral foundation so that we may more readily stand in the truth of our faith.

As we name and denounce the underlying beliefs that lead us astray, we untwist the cultural messages we have internalized. Doing so enables us to affirm the right impulses behind practices like IVF and surrogacy, for example, and redirect those impulses in a way that respects our human dignity and honors the sovereignty of God. We become free to act in a way that is in accord with our proper end.

Our underlying beliefs about reality determine the trajectory of our actions. As Catholic Christians, we are the stewards of enduring truths about who humans are and where we are going: We were made for heaven. As Saint Augustine so famously proclaims, "You have made us for yourself, O Lord, and our heart is restless until it rests in you."[3] We are not self-made creatures; we were made with a purpose. Our truest happiness lies in becoming who we are made to be and, by so doing, returning to Our Father. We know our end destination, and God in His mercy has revealed to us the path by which we get there. He Himself became the road!

As we approach the bioethical issues that are redefining motherhood and the family, it is imperative that we recognize the interrelated web of beliefs beneath the surface. The drastically different conclusions we reach on questions of ethics, of how to behave, arise out of different beliefs about who we are and what we are meant to be. Here, briefly, are a few of the twisted messages we must unravel if we are to allow the true beauty of the Church's vision for the moral life to inform our thinking:

The Culture's Message	The Church's Vision
We can be whatever we wish.	We are finite creatures; there is a vision and purpose for our being that lies outside of ourselves.
We will be happy when we finally get *whatever* we want.	We become happy by being who we are made to be and in union with God.
Life is about self-fulfillment.	Life is about self-gift.
This life is all there is.	The fullness of our lives is in heaven.
We can and must be satisfied in the here and now.	This life is only a foretaste of the world to come.
Our subjective experience *is* reality.	We each subjectively experience part of an objective reality outside of ourselves.
There is no universal moral truth.	Moral truth exists to guide us in becoming who we are made to be.

We are most free when we have more options.	We are most free when we can easily do what is truly good.
Control over our lives belongs to us.	Control over our lives belongs to God.
Peace lies in nonconflict; everyone should be left to do as they wish.	Peace lies in surrendering ourselves to God's will.
Freedom consists in having few rules, impositions, or restrictions.	Freedom consists in having knowledge of what is good and the virtue to act accordingly.
The best outcomes are what alleviate suffering and create the most pleasure.	The best outcomes ensure the possibility of full flourishing for every single person.
Suffering is meaningless and must be avoided.	We can draw meaning and purpose from suffering.
The material world matters little.	The material world belongs to God and is a gift we must steward.
Our *selves* lie in our minds; our bodies are merely vehicles by which we experience pleasure or pain.	Our bodies are truly ourselves, in union with our minds.
We ought to treat each person as he wishes to be treated.	We ought to treat others as we wish to be treated.
Helping others makes us happy.	We help others because each person has dignity in and of himself.

At different times, we might locate our own behaviors or thought processes as springing from any place on this chart. Notice the different patterns arising out of each constellation of beliefs. The first column focuses on control, self-determination, and achieving certain ends. It is hard to see how this worldview is compatible with any real peace, hope, joy, or love. The second column allows for surrender, for accepting the cup of suffering. The postures are different: The ideas in the first column promote grasping, while those in the second column encourage receiving. In the first worldview, morality is seen as consisting primarily of rules and duties; increasingly, our culture rejects this sort of morality because it rightly intuits that being a good person is about more than following a list of rules. The worldview encompassed by the second column interprets morality more broadly, including rules as an essential part of the lifelong journey to grow into a person of virtue. Thus, morality is not blind obedience to a set of cultural mores but a repeated exercise of the will that shapes our character to act in accord with objective duties. The second column illustrates the Christian ideal; it describes the attitudes of the saints.

The culture's message is very inward-focused. That is what sin does: It turns us inward on ourselves. In this list of presuppositions, there is little space for communion or connection. When we seek to be our own gods, as the first column details, we close ourselves off from one another. This fails to satisfy us because we are not gods; we are made in God's image. And God, as we know, is a *com-*

munion of persons. Our goal as Christians is to move out of a self-focused way of living and become more free to give of ourselves as we were made to do, to root our decisions in the Church's vision more often than not. Thus, reliable principles of the moral life — principles designed to guide us to become more fully who we are made to be — must guide us deeper into communion with one another. The goal is not to become independent but to recognize our radical dependence on one another, to serve one another in joy, and, in so doing, to come to the fullness of love.

Tracing the Legacy of the Sexual Revolution

The words of Pope St. Paul VI's 1968 encyclical *Humanae Vitae* loom prophetic as we inherit the fruits of the Sexual Revolution more than fifty years later. In predicting a decline in respect for women, an increase in marital infidelity, and state imposition of mandatory contraceptive use as a means of population control, Pope Paul VI foresaw many of the factors that have destabilized the family, disrupting our society at its most basic level. As he predicted, widespread acceptance and use of contraception severed the important link between sexuality and procreation — or rather, it masked the *perception* of this indissoluble link in our cultural awareness. And because every form of contraception has a failure rate, contraception cannot be relied upon to provide its intended outcome without its malevolent counterpart, abortion. In its fight for the flourishing of every woman, the Women's Movement was seduced by the illusion of sex without consequences, and a generation of women was sold the lie that abortion was necessary for their equality with men — necessary and therefore good for women. The result: Our culture now embraces a view of women that disconnects motherhood from women's identity. This disconnect is fatal.

The denigration of motherhood is an attack on the family and on women themselves; regardless of whether she is called to the vocation of bringing up children, motherhood is central to the identity of every woman. When we begin seeing motherhood as something women *do* rather than something central to who they *are*, we lose the sense of the sanctity of this sacred calling. Rather than a holy mission, care of children and the family becomes just one line item among others on a list of a woman's priorities. Her deep instinct to respond attentively to the needs of those around her becomes an impulse she must stamp out to get ahead. This abandonment of motherhood does not enhance women's worth, but instead it relegates what is uniquely feminine to our sexuality alone.

We see evidence of this as the use of pornography rises and casual sex has become the norm. Women's increased presence in the workplace has yet to make it a truly hospitable environment for their flourishing, as success often requires that women's bodies mimic those of men. Women are expected to cut themselves off from their own fertility through contraception or abortion in order to achieve serious career advancement. As reproductive technology develops, women have been so alienated from their own motherhood that they are willing to offer their reproductive capacities for hire, even "donating" their own flesh and blood, their eggs, in addition to serving as incubators for a child that will become someone else's in the act of surrogacy. US regulations on commercial surrogacy are being relaxed. In vitro fertilization (IVF) is being embraced not just as a treatment for infertility, a backup plan, but as a "Plan A" as high-power employers encourage women to freeze their eggs to delay childbearing until after their careers have been established. We are on the cusp of fully decoupling reproduction and motherhood, attempting to wrest control out of God's hands and place it squarely in our laboratories. There is even a budding "sterilization movement" growing in popularity with Millennial women who have been encouraged to regard pregnancy and childbirth not as some of women's greatest capacities, but as dangerous burdens that are inherently unsafe.

We have relegated childbearing to the arenas of rights and the marketplace on the premise that anyone who desires to become a parent ought to be one. This is a bizarre and inconsistent notion, given the stringent standards we apply to would-be adoptive parents. The language of rights can never apply to the bearing and raising of children, because the reality is that no one has the right to the existence of another person. Power this great is tantamount to slavery. When we create children to satisfy the desires of their parents, we dehumanize these children and the women who bear them.

Chapters 2 through 11 of this book explore how our

culture rejects the sovereignty of God in our practices surrounding gender, sexuality, marriage, family, childbirth, infant nourishment, parenting, and the use of reproductive technologies. The bioethical issues interwoven with these uniquely human topics are fruitful ground for exploring who we are meant to be. In the chapters that follow, we will unpack the underlying narratives that lead to the conclusions that conflict with the Church's teachings, ultimately to defend her prescriptions as leading to our ultimate good.

Let us begin our exploration of our motherhood by answering the invitation to embrace our nature as embodied, gendered creatures.

CHAPTER 2

Male and Female
He Created Them

If we are to truly understand and embrace motherhood, we must first recognize it as rising out of our God-given feminine nature. Motherhood is the fullness of womanhood. While this was once easy to recognize and understand, we have come to a point where such a claim requires explanation. This chapter attempts to situate motherhood within the reality of our nature as enfleshed, gendered beings created to glorify and image God in a particular way: as women. Pope St. John Paul II wrote extensively during his pontificate about this very gift we have as women, calling it the *feminine genius*. This chapter explores the feminine genius, the status of the feminine in contemporary culture and how we have arrived here, and the necessity of embracing the unique contributions and genuine complementarity of the two genders.

Femininity Exists

Thinking back to chapter 1, how did you feel reading about our call as women to imitate Mary through *deference*? If we're honest, there's a part of us that bristles at the suggestion that attributes like humility and obedience are part of our innate identity as women. We have been socialized to reject these qualities, once considered true gifts of our feminine nature. We have been sold the lie that these traits are not good, that the masculine gifts are what are truly valuable, and that equality with men means pursuing *their* qualities. Gifts more natural to us, those feminine in nature, we have been taught to despise as the tools of our own subjugation.

Our hearts still recognize the truth, though. In the depths of our souls, we cannot deny the witness that St. Teresa of Calcutta and Servant of God Dorothy Day, or even secular figures like Princess Diana and Eleanor Roosevelt, embody for us. These women lived the feminine genius, showing us what it means to be image bearers *as women* in our world. Our hearts still perceive the truth in joy, even as we have lost the language to express exactly what it is that we are seeing.

Few would deny that there is a brokenness between men and women today. After many centuries of societal imbalance, of men abusing their masculinity to keep

women out of societal arenas of power, the last century has
seen a swift and dramatic shift in how men and women relate to one another. Some of these shifts — such as greater
opportunities for women in education, government, and
the workplace — have been crucial reparations for cen-
turies-old imbalances. Others, though, have missed the
mark, creating new problems and inciting deeper hostil-
ity and alienation. Certainly we ought to denounce poor
manifestations of masculinity and femininity such as *ma-
chismo*, toxic masculinity, and toxic femininity.

What becomes problematic is a response that denies
the *existence* of a true masculinity and femininity altogether, rather than merely decrying these examples as the
poor exemplars they are. We see deep confusion reflected
in our current debate over the very existence and number of genders. Our culture has become so steeped in the
narrative that our minds and our subjectivity have the
power to create reality that we no longer maintain faith
in what we can see and touch as testifying to the truth.
Our children grow up and no longer trust their own bodies to tell them something of their identity. We no longer
understand clearly what it means to be a man or a woman,
and we have become so confused as to think that this is
a problem that can be fixed by a rearranging of our flesh
— as though adding a tail and some whiskers could make
us a cat. When we mistrust matter or separate the material from the spiritual world, inevitably we prize spirit over
matter — mind over flesh. To some degree, it is part of the
Christian ethos to privilege spiritual matters over earthly

ones. It is quite another thing altogether to deny objective reality, to ignore what science tells us about the human body, and to refuse to accept the testimony of the physical world altogether — that, indeed, is madness.

Femininity, Suppressed

In recent years, the number of movies with female leads has increased dramatically. Some see this trend as positive, but a close look at the way these women are portrayed reveals that they are hardly ever authentically feminine characters — that is, these characters fail to act in ways that reveal the heart of a woman or embody the feminine genius. This is particularly true of the female leads in superhero and other action franchise films. Beyond costumes with exaggerated emphasis on the physical parts distinct to female bodies, little about these female leads is feminine. The plot lines, battle scenes, and character development leave aside struggles and interests that are unique to women.

While critics have cheered as Katniss, Wonder Woman, Black Widow, and Captain Marvel graced the silver screens and have touted them as signs of progress, one has to wonder: What exactly is the nature of this progress? If we are to cheer for the genuine advancement of women, shouldn't we applaud stories that resonate with real women? The women in these films are interchangeable with men. If we could replace these leading ladies with male actors with little but a costume change necessary to make the story work, we can hardly call this progress for women. These characters are effectively men in the bodies of women. As audience members, we are meant to cheer as men pummel these women, as though this is some kind of progress. This is not what our world or our young girls should aspire to become. What we need to see is women triumphing *as women*.

In contemporary entertainment, women are asked to play all the roles, but only as deeply masculine or as a harlot. Motherhood is continually depicted as an obstacle to fulfillment. Women are portrayed as both the breadwinners and the boo-boo kissers of the family. Men, on the other hand, are written as licentious boys, nefarious villains, or, at best, oafish louts whose attempts at living with real meaning are worthy of mockery and disdain. *Stand back*, is the message of these films to men, *you are not necessary. Women can do it all, and do it better than you.*

We are tempted to reject authentic femininity because we have been taught that what is feminine isn't valuable. Want proof? How does your gut react to this list of feminine gifts: docility, kindness, gentleness, humility, nurture? Do these qualities strike you as attractive? Useful? They certainly are if we hope to get to heaven! We have been socialized not into gender roles, as sociologists claim, but into the rejection of those qualities that are uniquely feminine, and into prizing and chasing masculine strengths instead. As women increasingly embody masculine qualities, they attempt to prove their worth to men by becoming men. Yet, women's impersonation of men stunts both genders, encouraging men to abandon their pursuit of heroic masculine virtue by way of sexual license, which in turn locks them into eternal boyhood. This attitude furthers the chasm between men and women by perpetuating the use and objectification of women as men pursue a see-want-consume approach to relationships.

Cultural Roots, Cultural Fruits

Where does all of this come from? How has it taken root so deeply in today's culture? It has its origins in the laudable attempt to right the historical wrongs done to women, to bring them into their proper place as equals alongside men. In the United States, the Women's Movement and the accompanying Sexual Revolution emphasized women's equality with men through "sameness." That is, this movement and its propaganda communicated the biblical message that men and women are equal in dignity through a very misguided principle: Women are and can be just like men, and in order for equality to come about, women must pursue and achieve the same goals as men. In order for women to be on par with men, they had to be allotted the space to pursue careers, advancement, and power in the same ways and to the same degrees as men. Rather than asking what is unique about women and what support women need so that they can pursue full flourishing *as women*, this movement insisted that women's unique gifts and needs be muted to fit more easily into the existing structures. Unfortunately, contemporary secular femin*ism* denigrates the femin*ine* so that even praising qualities like gentleness and receptivity is viewed with suspicion. With comical irony, secular feminism has lifted up masculinity as the height of humanity, effectively erasing the feminine genius from our cultural mindset. Forcing women into a male mold is much easier than asking how educational, governmental, and corporate structures might be reshaped to accommodate women, and it is certainly easier on the bottom line.

What might a society reshaped by the feminine genius look like? As Pope Francis has declared, "The feminine genius is needed wherever we make important decisions."[1] Concretely, the types of changes women might wish to enact could include maternity leave during doctoral studies. Mothers might ask for work accommodations, such as remote work opportunities, flexible hours, and lengthier periods of paid maternity leave. Women might remake places of work to more fully address the needs of employees or enact benefits such as on-site childcare. Advocates could implore governments to offer more support to young mothers who are struggling. These are important examples of how the feminine genius might reshape our world into a more hospitable and joy-filled place. Clearly, many options allowing for women's full inclusion come with higher price tags than the current standard of neutralizing women's fertility through contraception and abortion.

Although it was a cheap and expedient path to increasing the number of doors open to women, the stamping out of women's fertility has not proven to be the equalizer it was sold as. A society that welcomes women only insofar as it mutes their life-giving capacities is one incompatible with their full flourishing. As women, when we strive for equality by approximating "sameness" with men, we deny what makes us uniquely feminine. Rather than society reshaping the workplace to be more hospitable to women and their desire to become mothers, women must reshape their bodies to resemble those of men: fruitless and barren.

And we are becoming so. As women delay childbearing to pursue educational and career goals, infertility rises due to advanced maternal age; the effects of sexual promiscuity, including sexually transmitted diseases; long-term contraceptive use; and the effects of abortions. Delayed childbearing and the use of formula also introduce greater health risks to women, as evidenced by the protective effects of breastfeeding under the age of thirty (see chapter 7). It appears that time spent breastfeeding positively correlates with decreased risk of breast and ovarian cancers.

Attempts to fix the problems of women's equality through contraception and abortion have strangled feminine flourishing (see chapter 4). The idea that women enjoy "sexual freedom" without consequence, as men so long have, is laughable. In place of women's freedom, these "solutions" have brought about a culture in which our femininity has been reduced to our sexuality. No longer is the sexual act regarded as a sacred gift of a woman to a man, nor is it seen as a prize worthy of protection. No, now sex has become a mutual masturbatory experience that is sometimes traded for dinner but often called up nearly anonymously through apps that allow partners to treat sex as casually as a handshake, a mere scratching of an itch they cannot reach.

But men and women are not *different,* we have been conditioned to object. *Any woman can do anything a man can do, just as well or better.* While personality traits differ for each singularly unique human soul, we surrender a great gift and beauty when we deny the existence of innate ontological differences between men and women. These qualities are God-given strengths, ways our Creator blesses the world uniquely through us. When we reject gender differences as merely socialized roles or stereotypes, we lose important guideposts toward becoming our truest selves. When we deny those qualities that are uniquely feminine, the whole of our difference is relegated to our sexual organs, to our genitalia. If we have been socialized into anything, it is to deny the value of our own femininity and to despise men's attempts to embody the masculine qualities that our femininity calls forth. Secular feminism scoffs at gallantry, from the glow of pride in a husband who sees himself as the provider to the merest gesture of a gentleman who offers his seat to a woman on the subway or who has the audacity to hold the door for her.

Somewhere along the way, women bought the lie that the inequalities and discrimination they faced were the result of feminine qualities, and that what women needed, therefore, was to become less womanly. Thus began the attempt of the feminist agenda to lift up women by helping them to become more like men. For any true flourishing of women to occur, we need a countermovement, one that elevates rather than denigrates authentically and uniquely feminine strengths.

The Feminine Gifts and Abilities

When we lose our sense of the particularity of masculinity and femininity, we also lose an essential component of our journey to sainthood. Sainthood is about becoming most fully ourselves, and we, as mothers, were created to fulfill that identity uniquely as women. To identify the particular does not deny the existence of a whole, and so to name the feminine gifts does not discount that an individual woman may have particular gifts in an area we normally understand to be an area of masculine strength. St. Joan of Arc is a good example of this. Through her courage and strength of conviction, she became a hero in the Hundred Years' War between France and England. But it is important to note that her feminine genius was essential to answering God's call; not once did she fight in combat or kill an opponent, though she led men into battle. Still, Joan is one female saint among thousands. God can and does work in extraordinary ways, but more often He chooses to work through ordinary and simple means. And so, it behooves us to offer our cooperation with those means — in this case, learning to love and embody more fully those feminine gifts that He has written into our souls. It is imperative that we reject attempts to deny gender differences if we are to become truly whom God has made us to be.

Recognizing that there are distinct ontological differences between men and women helps us find joy in the pursuit of our respective identities and in the complementarity of these gifts in the family and in society. While we think of the role of mother as primarily within the family context, the identity of mother is written into the feminine soul. Motherhood is the central aspect of the feminine genius, the relational role we hold with respect to the rest of the human family. The work of the feminine genius is to care, nurture, and welcome. We make space at the table. Men sacrifice, protect, and provide *at our insistence.* As we grow in our own capacity for care, attentiveness, and nurture, we invite men to respond. Our vulnerability invites men to action. Think of how peasants of old appealed to the queen for charity. If moved, the queen, in turn, would influence her husband toward charitable policies and attentiveness to the needs of his people. In this dynamic, a woman calls a man's attention to a particular cause, and he, for her sake, attends to that need. More humorously, this dynamic appears in the popular film *My Big Fat Greek Wedding,* when Toula's father refuses to give her his blessing to marry her fiancé, who isn't Greek. Toula appeals to her mother, who insists that although the man is the head of the family, the wife is the neck, and the neck "can turn the head any way she wants." Women, naturally attentive to the personal, perceive and draw attention to needs that might otherwise be missed.

Various thinkers have offered observations about what the feminine gifts may be. Pope St. John Paul II often highlighted receptivity and attentiveness to the personal in his writings on women. Alice von Hildebrand's writings identified purity and docility to God's word as central to the identity of women. Whichever characteristics we name, we ought to be mindful that naming any one trait as a masculine or feminine gift is *not* saying that individuals of either gender necessarily share or do not share in that particular trait. Nor are we speaking about particular skills, such as mathematical reasoning or aptitude for baking or driving a car. No, these gifts speak to the relational dimensions of our personhood, and understanding them provides us with insight into our own identity and the modes by which we offer ourselves in self-gift. We are reminded that "man, who is the only creature on earth which God willed for itself, cannot fully find himself except through a sincere gift of himself."[2] Becoming aware of our gifts can help us strengthen those unique capacities so that we are working with our nature, rather than against it.

The unique gifts of men and women are not limited to the spiritual. Indeed, some of women's most awe-inspiring capacities are written into our bodies. Leah Jacobson, author of *Wholistic Feminism*, identifies the distinctly feminine abilities of ovulation, gestation, and lactation, drawing attention to the fact that, despite their profound and almost "superhuman" power of bringing forth and nurturing new life, women's bodies have been routinely marginalized and denigrated in our society:

> We've allowed our culture to blame our bodies for all the inequalities we experience as women. In every woman's magazine, there are multiple articles that communicate our worth in terms of our sexual appeal, our careers, and our freedom from long-term commitments such as marriage and

children. The single, sexually available woman is portrayed as the height of happiness and success. The only mention of our feminine abilities is in ads for ovulation-suppressing drugs, information on delaying pregnancy, and virtually nothing about our breasts lactating, except a million tips on maximizing breast cleavage with the WonderBra and makeup tricks. *Rather than elevating culture to appreciate and support women's bodies, we settled for a culture that says our bodies are for sexual pleasure only, making the right to alter, suppress, and destroy our fertile, life-giving female bodies the supreme "women's" right.*[3]

If this is the environment in which we are raising our daughters, in which we ourselves have been raised, is it any wonder that so many millions of teens and grown women struggle with anxiety, eating disorders, and body image issues?[4] Has the expansion of so-called women's freedom, brought about by greater access to contraceptives and abortion, served to improve the situation? Even much-lauded attempts to establish healthier conceptions of women's bodies in advertising, such as Dove's Real Beauty campaign, fall painfully short of recognizing what is truly incredible about the female form. By continuing to focus narrowly on appearance and emphasize suppression or elimination of the feminine abilities through contraception and abortion, we perpetuate, rather than ameliorate, the systemic injustices women face as a result of the natural differences between their bodies and those of men. Rather than dampening the feminine abilities and remaking female bodies to mimic men's, we ought to focus on efforts to reshape society to accommodate and celebrate these female "superpowers" (for more, see chapter 4).

Femininity, Erased

We need not scour headlines for evidence of the unique gifts and abilities of women being suppressed or commandeered. Far from recognizing the wisdom written into our bodies, our culture's latest fad is to deny the realities of these bodily differences altogether. In a series of bizarre efforts made ostensibly in the interest of equality, women's unique needs and concerns are being systematically erased across cultural arenas from medicine to the sports field. In order to pacify transgender advocates, medical journals and even the CDC have begun eliminating gender-specific language from their literature — even when that language has very real consequences for medical treatment and decisions. Women are now being referred to as "bodies with vaginas" and "pregnant people."[5] Grace Emily Stark points out what is at stake when we remove female-specific language from our cultural mindset: "In our rush to be inclusive and sensitive in our language, we see a subtle erasure of the humanity, the very personhood, of women ... if biological men can acquire facsimiles of ... female body parts, and we agree, as a culture, that by definition this makes them women, what incentives will there be to protect the very real vulnerabilities and unique health needs of biological women?"[6]

Stark's words are not a slippery slope argument but an accurate description of how the protected status that women still enjoy in the developed world continues to erode. As transgender swimmer Lia Thomas, a biological male, is lauded by the media for "shattering records" in women's swimming at the University of Pennsylvania,[7] the true absurdity of defining men and women by some process of internal deliberation — rather than by the concrete, scientific, and empirically observable differences that separate them — is manifest openly. This is not an isolated incident, but merely one of many instances in which the "accomplishments" of biological males are eclipsing those of women who attain true excellence in their fields. And yet espousing the view that men and women's biologically endowed physical characteristics are different enough to warrant separate competitive arenas in this culture is enough to find oneself labeled a bigot.

As if it were not enough to erase women from scientific literature or crowd them out of their competitive arenas, some researchers are currently working toward helping men to commandeer feminine abilities for themselves. While much of the research to date has revolved around using these techniques to restore functioning to women's bodies, many hope for its implementation in the male population, particularly for gay and trans men hoping to reproduce without the assistance of surrogate "gestators" (although as we will see in chapter 11, technologies are developing such that we may not need to rely on the abilities or genetics of a particular gender to reproduce in the future).

Efforts are now underway to make possible uterine transplants and lactogenesis to enable men to gestate and nurse infants. Journal authors discuss possible methods to induce "chestfeeding" for biological males who have reproduced via surrogacy[8] (because apparently the term "breast" is now offensively gender-specific), and Chinese researchers celebrate the first live births by male mice via uterine transplant and IVF.[9] Although still in the experimental stages, uterine transplant research necessitates the removal of women's wombs from their bodies to be inserted into those of men in a stitching together of bodies that would have Mary Shelley shaking in horror.

Gender Complementarity and the Family

The growing trend to deny gender differences has radical implications for the family. Without a true sense of masculinity and femininity, it becomes difficult to articulate the value of motherhood and fatherhood because any flavor of parental love will do. The central question ought not to be, "What feels fulfilling to the parents?" but instead, "What is best for the children?" The studies support what we know to be true: Children need a mother *and* a father. Single parenthood is linked to adverse outcomes for children, such as greater likelihood of arrest, greater likelihood of abuse of drugs and alcohol, and higher rates of dropping out of school.[10] The gifts and complementarity of both sexes are essential to the well-being and development of the child. Acknowledging these facts (and they are facts) does not diminish the real love of joy-filled families in nontraditional configurations, nor is one configuration a guarantee of better outcomes than another. Knowing that there is an ideal in which children flourish best does not limit the power of God to work in all circumstances.

This knowledge serves not as a judgment of particular family situations, but as a tool by which we can intentionally make decisions about how to structure the human family *when it is within our power to do so.* For example, knowledge gleaned from these studies might bolster a spouse to persevere in pursuing an amicable marital relationship despite serious breaches of vows, such as infidelity, for the sake of the children's well-being. On the other hand, a widower — rather than trying to become both mother and father to his children — might move in with his children's grandmother to ensure a consistent motherly presence in his children's lives. Knowing the truth about which conditions lead to the best outcomes can support families in their discernment of the best possible situation taking into account the particular circumstances of their present moment.

Knowledge of the unique impacts of mothers and fathers also ought to inform how we think about creating families. Many women, feeling in themselves a deep desire for motherhood, might wonder about intentionally pursuing single parenthood through artificial insemination of donor sperm. To intentionally conceive a child in such a circumstance, however, violates the right of the child to be raised with both parents.[11] Already, this action introduces disorder into the parent-child dynamic by making the child the object of the fulfillment of his parent's desires (see chapter 10 for a deeper discussion on artificial reproduction). A more generous path might be to pursue other opportunities for self-gift such as foster care, missions work, or volunteering where existing needs for love are currently going unmet.

In the decades since the Sexual Revolution, our society has asked women to imitate and strengthen masculine qualities, and so we, as a culture, have been thrown out of balance. We need the complementarity of masculinity and femininity for healthy marriages, families, and societies. We need it in our Church. God created both genders with unique gifts meant to embody, each working in tandem with the other, with roles as specific and as intertwined as the chambers of the human heart. The heart both pushes out oxygenated blood to feed the entire human body and receives blood back into itself. If either side of the heart is weakened, the other must work harder; this throws the heart out of balance, damaging it and creating toxicity for the whole body. Recovering a sense of our own identity as women and grounding ourselves in the fullness of truth about who we are, inclusive of our embodied nature, is essential. When we cease trying to be everything, we can finally and more effectively become who we really are. Accepting our finite and particular nature allows us to do our part and do it well, and to trust others to do the same.

In the end, understanding the complementarity of the sexes reveals to us in a deeper way the vital importance of both motherhood and fatherhood in our children's lives.

We see that in the interest of their well-being, we have a duty to ensure that children have the benefit of being raised in the context of a loving marriage and, if this is no longer possible, that the healthy influence of both sexes remains integral in their upbringing.

Recovering Femininity

The way to combat a vice is to perform acts of its opposite virtue. We combat cowardice with acts of bravery, and laziness with diligence. A society saturated with women's sexual characteristics but devoid of true femininity needs a dose of authentic womanhood. As women, we are called to nurture our spiritual motherhood in every facet of society. We can practice St. Francis de Sales' "true strength" of gentleness, bringing nurture and attention to particulars at the office and in our homes. We can remind ourselves and others of our sacred dignity, honoring our bodies through modesty of dress, which serves to direct attention to our whole person. Our femininity may be uncomfortable to explore, particularly if we have been socialized to denigrate the very qualities God designed to shine in us.

Men should never cease to be gentlemen, sacrificing themselves in order to show the protection, honor, and deference with which they were designed to treat women. If nothing else, the gallantry of these guardians of beauty will serve as a reminder to women of who they really are and long to be, even when they may have lost touch with it themselves.

Like the rest of us, our children were not designed to

"discover themselves" in isolation. As humans, we find ourselves through sincere gift of self to others, through relationships and the narratives we receive through those relationships. Our children are not islands unto themselves. Some parents believe that this is the case and take a hands-off approach, fearing that their influence amounts to undue pressure on their children to develop according to a particular school of thought. The reality is that we are designed to learn from one another. Our behavior will influence and teach our children whether we intend it to or not. If we take a hands-off approach, they learn to disregard our opinions and absorb the worldviews of those who are less timid. In a culture radically confused about the meaning of gender and sexuality, we have a wealth of clarity to offer our children, who need not grow up with the anxiety of determining even the most basic details of their identity that ought to be apparent. Our gender is not a "guess" made at birth, as some are beginning to claim, but a gift imprinted on our souls from the moment of our creation. We can teach our children to value whom they are and whom God has made each of us to be. And for those of us who have grown up female in a culture that denigrates all that is feminine, perhaps what we teach our children will free us to be more fully ourselves as well.

CHAPTER 3

Revisiting "Happily Ever After"

One of the most popular television shows of the last twenty years was the mockumentary *Modern Family*. As the title implies, the show made light of the contemporary American family in its myriad configurations, from a drastically younger "trophy" wife to gay adoptive uncles to a traditional couple with three children. *Modern Family* garnered the love of fans by showing the trials of family living in a humorous light. The real brilliance of the show, driving its eighty-five Emmy nominations and twenty-two wins, was its consistent return to the charming notion that love of family conquers all. In a time when more and more American homes are plagued by the pain and brokenness of divorce, separation, and single parent-hood, the Dunphys are a symbol of hope amidst modern challenges. Many viewers recognize themselves and their own families in the crazy drama of the Dunphys and embrace the message that, in the end, only love matters.

God's Plan for the Family

It is true that love is beautiful wherever it is found; it's also not the whole story. Remember the road trip metaphor from chapter 1: If heaven is our destination, then moral rules are our guide to getting there. The guidance of the Church helps us to find the surest, most expedient route. If we stray from this guidance, we may, after many twists and turns, happen upon the right road. But even if we do, it is likely that we will end up lost and frustrated many times along the way.

We have lost sight of the original meaning of the family as God intended it, as a reflection of Trinitarian love and communion. Time and again, Scripture draws on images of marriage to reflect the love and fidelity between God and His people, between Christ and His Bride. Marriage, Pope St. John Paul II tells us, is "the image and symbol of the covenant which unites God and His people,"[1] and children are "a permanent sign of [the] conjugal unity" of the spouses.[2] He clarifies that the central purpose of the family is to guard, reveal, and communicate love. He responds to those who claim that the doctrines of the indissolubility of marriage and the demand for total fidelity are "impossible" by affirming that it is by the grace of the sacrament, not the powers or limited will of the spouses, that married love is able to be what it is meant to be: the image of God's complete and irrevocable love for us.[3]

The Church's moral teachings surrounding dating and marriage are not oppressive; they are practical guidelines for living a happy life. Taking monogamy as an example, we can see that many years spent sleeping around make poor practice in the virtue of fidelity. Those who remain chaste practice fidelity to their future spouse, and so are well prepared for the challenges of married life. The availability of contraception in combination with the decline of social pressures to remain monogamous have left us with a society in which promiscuity and divorce make fidelity all the more challenging — when fidelity is attempted at all. As ideas of what is "ethical" shift away from duties and responsibilities and toward the thin notion of autonomous consent, younger generations are reviving the "free love" attitudes of the 1960s, promoting non-monogamous poly-amory that leaves each partner in a marriage more "free," as though mere agreement to permit infidelity could prevent the damage done to the bond between marital partners. Having fewer "rules" has not made us freer in the Christian sense of being enabled to more easily live a more virtuous life. Rather, the creation of an ideal family situation is less possible and less accessible, and finding a good partner is more difficult. Delays in childbearing are often less about women's self-actualization than they are the result of a less loving, less monogamous society. The growing phenomenon of redefining the family is born of desperation; women (and men) who lack hope that they can create an ideal child-rearing environment seek to create their own kind of family structure on terms more attainable to them within a reasonable amount of time.

Family life is meant to be a training ground of virtue. And certainly family comes in many configurations, sometimes dictated by circumstances beyond our control: A spouse may pass away or abandon us for addictions. Regardless, the insight of *Modern Family* remains true: Love can and does still bind families together. In *addition* to that truth, standing alongside it, remains the fact that love *thrives* under certain conditions — the conditions God created for us. When we lean into these conditions, when we assent to what God has revealed as His will for us, it is like using the best brand of motor oil to keep your car functioning. Sure, it might run into other problems, but if you want to do what you can as the owner to keep it running optimally for as long as possible, you need to follow the recommended maintenance schedule in the owner's manual.

Even when God's plan for the family makes sense to us, it can be less than compelling in light of so much evidence of love gone wrong even in "traditional" families and so much good apparent in families that don't measure up to the "ideal" standard. Particularly because we don't want to leave anyone out or hurt anyone's feelings, we are tempted to deny that any standard exists at all. All that matters, we think, is who is actually closest to the end game: whose family most clearly treats each other with unconditional love. That is a fair point. Human beings are resilient. The stories of the saints echo with the triumph of dark and difficult circumstances overcome.

When we talk about what is ideal for marriage and the family, it is not to discount the holiness and love that exist and even flourish under all sorts of circumstances. Rather, the ideal is the set of conditions under which we are most *likely* to flourish. What are the circumstances that make it easiest to build virtue, to love God and others, and to become saints? It is not a guarantee; we are all broken and need a Savior. But the fact remains that if we want to learn to love well, the family is where God intends us to study.

And what have we done to the family? Over the past sixty years, our society has done its best to devalue and dismantle the family. In chapter 4, we will look at the insidious ways contraception and abortion have aided and abetted this destruction. Here, we will look at the Christian ideal of family, how it's being dismembered, and what we need to do about it. If the family is "the most effective means for humanizing and personalizing society,"[4] as Pope St. John Paul II tells us, then it is imperative that we heal the brokenness of our families. It is not about accusing or demeaning families that don't measure up; none of us will. We ask the key question, *What are families meant to be?* so that we know toward what end we are striving. Only in this light can we explore questions about becoming a mother and understand which options are ethical in complex situations that are becoming ever more murky.

Reconfiguring the Family

Our individualism and warped notions of freedom (see chapter 1) have poisoned our views of love and of parenthood, essentially turning us in on ourselves. When we look for a partner or a child to satisfy ourselves, we will remain unsatisfied, and we will wound our loved ones in the process. "Happily ever after" *is* real. It just doesn't belong to this lifetime, nor is it something we can grasp. Rather, it is something we must receive. When we misguidedly place our hopes for happily ever after in a spouse or in our children, we miss the gift that they are: not the source of our happiness themselves, but the opportunity for real love to flourish when we pour ourselves out. Love creates community, and self-gift creates joy. And so the impetus to form a family ought never to be from a drive toward self-fulfillment, but rather from its opposite: a readiness to self-sacrifice as Christ commands us.

Our culture is writing a narrative that is altogether different. Over the last several decades, pop culture has seen a rise in film and television depictions of reconfigured families unbound from traditional structures. Romantic comedies such as *Knocked Up* and *Life as We Know It* explore what happens when children come not only prior to marriage but even prior to romantic involvement. Such storylines beg the question: Can the bond of parenthood *create* love between a man and a woman? The iconic television series *Friends* made light of surrogacy in its storyline about main character Phoebe carrying her brother's triplets. The message? Any and all configurations of the family are equally viable as a means to love. While this is a lovely sentiment, the real crux of the matter is not whether it makes us feel warm and fuzzy or if turning societal expectations on their head makes for better entertainment. What matters is the degree of truth a story holds. And while it is certainly true that where there is love, there is God, the creation and configuration of our families *matters.* Strategies of "anything goes" place the players and their potential flourishing in precarious positions. The fatal flaw in these depictions of parenthood and our society's philosophy of parenting at large is that both place the satisfaction of parental desires at the center, rather than the good of the children.

Unfortunately, the dismantling of the family has yanked reproduction from the arena of responsibility and placed it squarely within that of rights. Our thinking about parenting in general and motherhood specifically has become more about parental desire than anything else. The disrespect with which we have come to regard the human fetus has inevitably infected how we regard the children of this generation, the survivors of the abortion holocaust. As the fabric of the family is reduced to threads, so the dignity of children is coming unwound. Children are not gifts to be received but goods to obtain or even be made to order (see chapter 11 for what is coming to a baby factory near you). Parenthood is no longer a sacred duty carried out in partnership; now it is a status to be achieved to satisfy personal desire or fulfillment.

Sites and apps such as Modamily and Just a Baby serve

a vision of the family in which children are viewed as objects to be obtained. They attempt to create a marketplace in which one can "reimagine relationships"[5] in choosing a legal parenting partner rather than raising children within a loving family. Through egg and sperm "donation," biological parents abandon their relationship with the children their actions intend to create. (See chapter 10 for further discussion of these topics.) Single people can obtain children for the satisfaction of their desires as well. At best, this mentality places children in the category of pets. (Perhaps this is why we see the rise of phenomena like dog cupcake bakeries and terms such as "fur baby." We are terribly confused about the difference between an infant and a puppy.) Or perhaps parenting is akin to gardening: an activity one undertakes that, despite its being more serious and demanding than other pursuits, is ultimately a hobby. When children are commissioned rather than received, family is not the sacred place where children are stewarded as the living witnesses of the love of two parents become one.

The Real Purpose of Parenthood

This is not to say that traditional families are perfect or that their children do not in many ways fulfill the deeply held desires of their parents to have a family. What is at stake here is the dignity and well-being of the children who are intentionally brought into each of these configurations and the consequences of this redefinition of procreation for society as a whole. While there will always be happy exceptions to every rule, statistics overwhelmingly support a two-parent household as vital to positive outcomes for children, from better psychological and physical well-being to higher high school graduation rates.[6] From the view of the family as the Domestic Church and a training ground for virtue, we must treat our children as the gifts that they are if we are to resemble the Christian vision for the family (see chapter 4 for a discussion of the culture of hospitality).

What does it say about our society if we sanction the pursuit of parenting through practices that inherently disregard the dignity of children, regarding them as products for sale? What kind of relationship is parenthood? Is it stewardship of another person during his vulnerable years of growing in agency and character? Or is it for the fulfillment of our own desires? What is it we hope to accomplish when we actively pursue a parenting situation that puts the children at an overwhelming disadvantage to achieve a happy life?

Making the best of an existing situation — such as an unexpected pregnancy or suddenly necessary adoption — is laudable. *Creating* a less-than-ideal situation for the satisfaction of our own desires is selfish. If, from the outset, we seek to create "family" primarily for the personal gratification of the parents, the governing value of such a family becomes objectification rather than relationship.

The Christian view of family is radically different. As Pope St. John Paul II articulates, "Each member of the family has to become, in a special way, the servant of the others and share their burdens."[7] The family is where children are formed for their purpose in life. Each family is a Domestic Church in which children come to know their identity as beloved children of God, meant to grow in virtue and created for a life of union with Jesus.

God is the author of reality, and thus the concept of family can never be reduced to a mere contract. Apps claim to reduce the complication, confusion, and messiness of creating a family. In reality, they serve to aggravate the loneliness and disintegration so characteristic of our time. When children are sought as a means to fulfill their parents, they are, from their very conception, set up for failure. Our happiness is not found in the other, but rather in the pouring out of ourselves.

Living the Gospel through Family

As we will see in chapter 10, even the most basic roles of "mother" and "father" are being dismantled. In an unprecedented way, our reproductive practices require that we distinguish between motherhood that is biological, gestational, social, or some combination thereof. We have a schizophrenic relationship with biology, insisting it is not important in the case of abortion, surrogacy, or embryo adoption, but so vital as to warrant the expense and heartache of multiple IVF attempts.

As we think about practices that grow our families, we must keep our end in mind. Our decisions about how to structure our families, and when, whether, and with whom to bear children should correspond not to our immediate desires (although they do have value), but rather to our ultimate end: life in Christ. Single, divorced, infertile, stepparenting — no matter how you configure a Christian family, we cannot cease to be products of our own time and culture. Our goal as Christians on the pilgrimage to sainthood is not necessarily to reject this culture, but to navigate what living the Gospel looks like in this time and place, and to become witnesses of Christ's love to the world.

CHAPTER 4

Contraception
Versus a Culture
of Hospitality

For further evidence that madness has indeed gripped
our society, we need look no further than our largely
uncritical acceptance of the assumption that contraception is good for women. The Catholic Church has faced
substantial criticism throughout the past half century
as the lone prophetic voice decrying the societal harms
posed by contraception. As more evidence of the poison-
ous effects of contraception on women's health and status
begins to surface, more of us are beginning to recognize
contraception for the evil the Catholic Church has always

recognized it to be.

This chapter will detail the serious harms contraception does to women, children, their families, and society as a whole. Those who wish to promote contraception must acknowledge and grapple with these harms if they wish to fortify the view of contraception as a basic right of women. This view of contraception as a right stands not on solid science, but rather on the conditions that the widespread use of contraception itself creates. As we will see, these conditions are in themselves contrary to the good of women, and so the use of contraception perpetuates a society in which women's flourishing is diminished rather than ultimately supported. If there weren't a near conspiracy-level effort to ignore or even suppress the evidence against the use of hormonal contraceptives, perhaps by now we would have at our disposal a different way to regulate births, or, even better, a society that supports women in their natural state of fertility rather than insisting on the need to suppress it.

An Act of Surrender

"Every method of contraception has a failure rate," my OB reminded me. After experiencing life-threatening blood clots in my lungs during my second pregnancy, I was seeking her counsel on ways to avoid further pregnancies. The genetic condition that caused my clots is exacerbated by the hormones of pregnancy — incidentally, the same hormones used in birth control medications. These medications had already caused clots once before, when as a fresh college graduate I awoke on my first day of work to find my leg purple and quadrupled in size. What had once been the solution to my debilitating monthly cramps now put my life in peril as I rushed to the ER.

Until that point, I hadn't believed that the hormones I'd been pumping into my body since the age of thirteen could pose any real risk. As a teenage girl, I had trusted my doctors, and my mother agreed that the patches and the pills were the solution; the only person who had warned me about *any* kind of health risks associated with hormonal contraceptives was my eighth-grade Catholic school religion teacher. How differently things might have turned out if I'd given her enough credence to look into her claims. Years later, as I issued similar warnings in my own religion classroom, I wondered how many of my students were silently discounting me as I had my own teacher, even though I had a chilling visual of my own near-death experience to back up my claims.

But the moral cautions of the Church against hormonal contraceptives actually complement what science says about them. While they can drastically lower rates of conception (or, failing that, prevent healthy pregnancies from progressing), their efficacy in this arena comes with serious risks to women's health. Yet because the medical establishment and radical feminism have chosen to overlook these facts and instead insist that these medications constitute such a substantial good for women as to warrant their status as a basic right, I was left to learn about these risks the hard way.

And so, faced with the risks to my life and the very real possibility that my children might grow up without me, I found myself in my OB's office hoping the medical industry had developed some kind of miracle protection. Alas, things in the birth control world had not changed all that much since my teenage years. Hormones were out for me; their deadly potential was what I was trying to avoid in the first place. I was not open to the invasive, abortifacient, and possibly fertility-stealing effects of something like an IUD, nor was I willing to consider a final surrender of my fertility through sterilization. I'm not sure what I thought the doctor could give me. I knew there were no good options. I think I just wanted to feel less alone in deciding whether I was willing to risk the possibility of my children growing up without their mother. My husband and I had always imagined more children, but that dream felt irresponsible now. Didn't we have an obligation to avoid pregnancy in order to protect our kids?

The OB and I whittled the list down to condoms and other barrier methods — all of which were less effective than the Creighton Method of Natural Family Planning that my husband and I had been using since our engagement and up through that point. I walked out feeling angry that I had wasted my time on something I knew to be futile. And yet the doctor's words stuck with me: "Every method has a failure rate." The more I have considered these words, the more freedom I have found. The great burden of anxiety I felt over the decision to have more children stemmed in large part from society's mistaken idea that we have more control than we actually do. None of us is the author of life. Whether we conceive or not is ultimately not up to us. Of course, we can adjust our actions according to our intentions to achieve or avoid pregnancy, but conception itself is never fully within the control of the couple. That is where God's breath of creation meets the marital act. While there are indeed many considerations involved in growing our family (or not), the ultimate power in procreation lies with God. And it stays with Him, unless we wrest control away through sterilization or abstinence. The marital act is always an act of surrender, a fiat, a prayer: Let it be.

The paradox is that in this surrender I find the most freedom. Grasping at certainty is ultimately a futile endeavor. Much more life-giving is the acceptance of life's precarious nature. In this space there is room for faith in God's providence, in His plans for our family — faith that even when these plans may not hold what we would wish for ourselves, they hold something greater: that which corresponds to the true and ultimate good of our souls. This resonates all the more as we prepare to welcome baby number four, a little girl who will greet the world sometime between the editing and the publishing of this book. As an idea, a prospect, her existence held mostly fear and trepidation for me over daily injections, a risky delivery, and past birth trauma. But as my body expands and my children kiss my belly and squeal with delight when their baby sister responds to their voices through my tightly stretched skin , the light of joy shines so brightly that even the darkest corners of my soul warm through with love. It isn't the safest path we could have chosen. Nor is it likely to be the neatest, quietest, or most orderly. But we will undoubtedly walk it with greater love than we would have walked any alternative — love that, if we make it to heaven, will last for eternity.

As our daughter's namesake, Chiara Corbella Petrillo, wrote to the son for whom she forwent cancer treatments to save while he was in utero:

> Love is the center of our lives, because we are born from an act of love, we live for love and to be loved, and we die to know the true love of God. The goal of our life is to love and to be loved, always ready to learn how to love the others as only God can teach you. Love consumes you, but it is beautiful to die consumed, exactly like a candle that goes out only when it has reached its goal. Anything that you do in life will make sense only if you look at it in view of eternal life. If you are truly loving, you will realize this from the fact that nothing belongs to you, because everything is a gift.[1]

Is Contraception a Right?

Even as one half of an NFP-practicing couple, I fell prey to the illusory sense of control that our culture's use of contraception promotes. The widespread use of contraception has created a toxic assumption about our ability to sever the life-giving power from our sexuality, an assumption that is slowly poisoning our society. The fact is that contraception remains limited, able to prevent *most*, but not *all*, pregnancies. More accurate than the claim that contraception can "prevent" pregnancy is the statement that contraception *lessens its likelihood*. It is not helpful to speak as though contraceptives are truly able to prevent pregnancy; we ought to adjust our language to more accurately reflect contraception's limits. However, our society operates under the illusion that the moral responsibility of relationship with one's potential child and sexual partner can be erased through the use of contraception. But when contraception fails (as it often does — a failure rate of 1 percent taken monthly over ten years cumulatively becomes a whopping 70 percent), abortion can seem like a necessity to sexual partners unprepared and unwilling to become parents.[2]

This is where the language of "reproductive rights" has come into popular use. Many advocates of women's rights insist that access to contraception and abortion is a basic right to ensure that women, whose bodies bear an unequal burden in reproduction compared with those of men, do not face unequal consequences as a result. Assumed in this argument is the notion that men and women must be able to enjoy sex without hindrance. Perhaps if it really were true that contraception could completely sever the sexual act from its procreative powers, this might be a coherent notion. But as we have seen, that notion is merely an illusion.

No one can have a right to something that does not

exist, and so women and their supposed advocates cannot rightly claim access to technologies that divorce sex from its consequences as a right. Sex, like most relational human activities, has intrinsic consequences. The only sure way to avoid those consequences is to refrain from engaging in the act that causes them. To pretend anything else is to do a disservice to women. The assertion that contraception and abortion further women's health or flourishing is, as we will see, an outright lie. The fact is that far from being basic rights, these technologies damage women's physical and mental health, as well as their intimate and marital relationships, all while shaping a society that is less hospitable to their ultimate flourishing.

An Assault on Women

In addition to being a repetitive, or even daily, practice of closing oneself off to the possibility of new life, many methods of contraception are deeply damaging to women physically. Hormonal contraceptives are associated with increased risk for blood clots, breast and cervical cancer, human papillomavirus (HPV), osteoporosis, depression, anxiety, suicide, decreased libido, and increased susceptibility to developing autoimmune disorders.[3] On top of the increased risks for these myriad health concerns, "Hormonal contraception appears to put women into a physiological state of chronic stress, masculinizes their brains, and almost literally makes women different versions of themselves" by altering their perceptions of the world and their partners.[4] Hardly the path to women's liberation, contraceptives are damaging and, in some cases, even debilitating. Additionally, contraception contributes to increases in infertility by first delaying the average age of childbearing and then increasing levels of sexual activity, which in turn increases the likelihood of contracting fertility-damaging sexually transmitted diseases. Contraception is also bad for women because it encourages men to treat women (and themselves) poorly. The illusion of "safe" sex promotes promiscuity, adultery, prostitution, pornography, and abortion. Each of these is physically and emotionally damaging to women, risking their physical and mental health, their future fertility, and at times, their lives.

Poison to Marriage and Family Life

Contraception poisons marriage and parenthood by conditioning spouses for the use of one another and promoting antagonistic attitudes toward potential children. When we begin to believe and act as though the natural products of our sexuality — children — can truly be avoided, when we sever this sacred physical sign of spouses' mutual giving of themselves from its outcome — permanent, physical union — we desecrate ourselves. By neutering fertile ground, we reject the true gift of marriage: the full giving and receiving of self. When we ignore the spiritual reality that the momentary unity created in sex is meant to become a permanent physical reality, we objectify ourselves. We become less than what we are, and sex becomes a mere entwining of bodies rather than the joining of souls. In this way, sex becomes an activity which is aimed toward mere pleasure. Rather than deepening acceptance of our spouse and leading to greater unity, this mentality turns us inward on ourselves.

It wreaks havoc on a family dynamic when spouses have trained themselves to see children as inconvenient, as impediments. No doubt children really are these things. There is nothing convenient about waking up in the middle of the night to feed a newborn or comfort a sick child. Children are expensive and almost never pay their own way! Spouses who are open to life practice virtues that make them more prepared to welcome both planned and unexpected children. When spouses intentionally and habitually close themselves off to children, they make their family less hospitable to new life when it does come.

Abortion's Gateway Drug

All of the emphasis on ensuring the "safety" of sex presumes that women do not have the capability or will to constrain themselves from having sex. As recipients of the narratives about female sexuality presented in pop culture and public school health curricula, our daughters absorb the expectations that they will be sexually active and that contraception is a necessary tool for their health. Contraception, they are taught, is the responsible choice for a woman in today's society. This narrative fails to expose the myriad health risks, the risks to their plans for their future families, and, possibly most gaping of all, the utter inability of contraception to make good on its own promises.

The illusion that we can separate sexuality from procreation is the shaky foundation of what Pope St. John
Paul II termed the "contraceptive mentality," a view that
has created many cracks in the foundation of our society's
views on sexuality, childbearing, and the family. Pope
St. John Paul II described the results of this mentality in
Evangelium Vitae:

> Despite their differences of nature and moral grav-
> ity, contraception and abortion are often closely
> connected, as fruits of the same tree. ... Such prac-
> tices are rooted in a hedonistic mentality unwill-
> ing to accept responsibility in matters of sexuality,
> and they imply a self-centered concept of freedom,
> which regards procreation as an obstacle to per-
> sonal fulfilment. The life which could result from
> a sexual encounter thus becomes an enemy to be
> avoided at all costs, and abortion becomes the only
> possible decisive response to failed contraception.[5]

The contraceptive mentality inevitably leads to an abortive mentality at a societal level; abortion becomes "necessary" as a failsafe that would not be necessary in a society
where women are less pressured to be sexually active, better informed about contraception's real risks, and better
supported in motherhood when they do conceive and bear
children.

Many of the reasons people have for avoiding children
are serious — serious enough, in fact, that they should

avoid sex altogether. When we recognize that contraception merely lessens the *likelihood* of pregnancy, we see that unless we are willing to adjust our sexual behavior according to our readiness to accept parenthood as the natural consequence of sex, abortion becomes necessary to effectively eliminate the responsibility of parenthood. The more a society relies on contraception, the more it will inevitably rely on abortion.

In other words, contraception, in conjunction with unrealistic expectations about its ability to control a woman's fertility, leads to a culture in which abortion appears as a relief, a way out of a desperate situation. A society with fewer births and an increasingly narrow idea of who is responsible for the children born into it perpetuates conditions that make these difficult situations even more challenging.

The Gospel of Hospitality

The more we make use of contraceptive interventions as a society, the less free we are to avoid them. Fewer children in each family — fewer families, even — means a society less attentive to the needs of children and families. Many restaurants have become "grown-up" spaces. In some cities, it is easier to find a restaurant that welcomes dogs than it is to find one that welcomes children. Many supermarket chains are beginning to eliminate the children's seat at the front of their carts. Adult pools and child-free spaces are popular at luxury hotels and other recreational sites. Ultimately, contraception contributes to a culture that is less welcoming and at times downright inhospitable to children and families.

We see this mentality even in our churches. Some parishes include sweet letters in the bulletin welcoming families with young children and making allowances for the noise they naturally bring with them, reminding all parishioners that "if the Church isn't crying, it is dying." Others, however, fall prey to the contraceptive mentality that seeks to sanitize society of the inconveniences children pose. I attended a Mass recently where an announcement was made from the pulpit requiring that families with young children who "make noise" remain outside during the Mass. Barring children, most of whom are indeed baptized members of the Body of Christ, from the Mass is discriminatory. Not to mention that it flies in the face of the command given by Jesus himself when his apostles attempted to erect the same sort of barriers: "Let the little children come to me, and do not stop them; for it is to such as these that the kingdom of heaven belongs" (Mt 19:14). Perhaps we have something to learn about liturgy from those to whom the Kingdom truly belongs!

A society that is less hospitable to children ultimately becomes less hospitable to any and all vulnerability. As we grow less tolerant of dependence and weakness, we lose our pathways to empathy and connection. In reality, we all start life helpless. Society used to recognize the substantial debt that children owe their parents as they age. Increasingly, care of the elderly is relegated to facilities. This is due to many factors, including longer lifespans and more demanding care being both possible and necessary. But with fewer single-income families, it is also less possible for the most basic care to be rendered in the home by a devoted family member. Rather than being seen as a privilege in return for a lifetime of love, such care becomes regarded as a burden. The generations before us knew the value of their elderly. They also saw the value of children in the human community — they knew who would be taking care of them as they aged. Now, children and the elderly alike are viewed as an expensive nuisance. We routinely avoid and abort the children; it is only a matter of time before we legalize and institutionalize the disposal of our elderly as well.

This shift to seeing the weak and vulnerable as burdensome is one of the more prevalent currents in the tidal shift toward a culture of death. Among the top reasons for claiming the desire for assisted suicide is fear of becoming a burden.[6] Insurance policies for the elderly and dying are already coercively slanted against more expensive palliative and hospice care. It is financially preferable for patients to choose to expire expediently by making use of assisted suicide. In some cases, insurance companies are even refusing to cover life-saving care, opting to cover instead the more economic and efficient suicide drugs.[7]

We live in an age that assigns value only to productivity in the here and now. We have less respect for history and for the next generation. We have lost the art of hospitality and of welcoming the stranger. This is an attitude we have inherited from a contraceptive culture! We have received the message that our worth somehow depends on our performance, that we must contribute to be valuable. It is a cold and hellish society in which you must earn or demonstrate that you deserve your existence in some measurable way.

Thankfully, this is *not* the gospel message. The Christian worldview is to affirm the dignity of every human life without qualification. Psalm 128:3 speaks of the beauty of large families, likening children to olive plants around the table of a blessed father. Leviticus 19:34 urges the Hebrews to treat foreigners well, reminding them they were once strangers in Egypt. In the New Testament, Saint Paul commands hospitality in his Letter to the Hebrews, recalling that Abraham and Sarah "entertained angels without knowing it" by their welcoming of strangers (see 13:2). Jesus Himself reminds us that how we care for "the least of these" is how we care for Him (Mt 25:40). Scripture is a treasure trove of beautiful literature extolling the great blessing children are and reminding us of our duty to remain welcoming to the unexpected visitors in our lives.

While there may be good financial, medical, or psychological reasons for families to try to space births, the impetus behind contraception ultimately flies in the face of gospel values. The various forms of contraception seek, in fact, to create barriers to life. They seek to render a woman infertile, to make a mother's womb inhospitable even to life already conceived.

Embracing Fertility, Embracing Women
When there are legitimate reasons for couples to space

births, the Church promotes the use of Natural Family
Planning (NFP), or fertility awareness-based methods
(FABMs). Bring this up to your OB, and you are likely to
be faced with condescension and derision (ask me how I
know). The unfortunate reality is that most medical education and research regarding female fertility tends to
revolve around the interests of the pharmaceutical industry, to which contraceptives contribute a $7 billion an-
nual share in the United States alone.[8] Although medical
advances have yielded highly accurate methods of family planning, including symptothermal, cervical mucus,
and symptohormonal monitoring methods, their total
exclusion from medical education has resulted in generation after generation of clinical women's health providers
who are entirely uninformed, fallaciously equating them
with the debunked "rhythm method" and scoffing at the
well-demonstrated fact that these methods are as or more
accurate than the leading methods of hormonal contraceptives.[9] Suppressing a woman's fertility is immensely
profitable; there is relatively little to be gained, financially
speaking, in seeking alternatives that promote and work
with a woman's fertility.

While it can be tempting to read something systematic and malicious into the lack of true understanding
of FABMs on the part of medical providers, the reality
is that we are all products of our own environments and
biases. After sometimes decades of medical education
and clinical experience, it takes an open-minded individual to question the assumptions built into the exist-

ing paradigms of women's health and discover the truth, both about the harm contraceptives pose to women and the natural alternatives for family planning available to them. With billions of dollars creating a vested interest in maintaining the status quo of a societal and medical dependence on a fertility-suppressing system, it will take a substantive grassroots effort for women and their advocates to make their voices heard that women's bodies are not broken. Fertility is not a problem to be solved but a gift to be stewarded. Natural methods of family planning are more respectful of women's bodies, serving to honor and support the feminine abilities (see chapter 2) rather than mute and erode them.

In addition to supporting women, NFP furthers the good of the marital relationship. To use NFP effectively to space births, couples must communicate frequently about their ability to welcome more children into the family and decide together whether to abstain. This constant communication — in conjunction with the openness to life NFP fosters and evidence that couples with more children have lower divorce rates — may contribute to the lowered divorce rates among couples who practice NFP.[10]

NFP is also vital to the spiritual lives of married persons in living out the grace of the sacrament. Pope St. John Paul II explains that, through NFP, couples act "as 'ministers' of God's plan" by respecting the unitive and procreative aspects of sexuality that "God the Creator has inscribed in the being of man and woman and in the dynamism of their sexual communion."[11] By contrast, contraception achieves the end of spacing births through methods contrary to God's plan. Though the ends are the same, through the means of contraception, couples, "act as 'arbiters' of the divine plan and they 'manipulate' and degrade human sexuality — and with it themselves and their married partner — by altering its value of 'total' self-giving."[12]

The most genuine way for a couple to live out God's plan for marital love is by total acceptance of the other — acceptance that may require periodic times of abstinence from sex. Whether it comes after the birth of a child, in the midst of a serious illness, or during a prolonged separation such as military deployment, all marriages will encounter circumstances in which abstinence becomes necessary. The periodic abstinence practiced by NFP-using couples reinforces virtues that will help them faithfully weather the inevitable occasions when they will be unable to partake in conjugal union. Such restraint is far from easy. Given the stakes, though, we cannot pretend that contraception poses any sort of "solution," nor indeed anything less than a grave threat to women, their marriages, and their children.

Turning the Tide of a Contraceptive Culture

The reality is this: Sex is "safest" in a monogamous, covenantal marriage that is open to life. Our daughters need to have all the information: Far from being "safe," contraception damages their health, rewires their brains, and contributes to what Pope St. John Paul II termed the culture of death. It is not naive to promote abstinence education. Our children are not now, nor have they ever been, incapable of self-restraint. Indeed, for much of human history, a high level of control over one's sexual behavior was the expected social norm. Furthermore, in this current generation, we see trends of decreasing sexual activity.[13] Our children have all the information they want at the tips of their fingertips. What they lack, and what we can provide, is the wisdom necessary to sort through it. We can provide them solid ground on which to sort through this information and context in which to make prudent decisions.

We need greater transparency about the damaging effects of contraceptives: the mechanisms by which they prevent births, the risks they pose to our daughters' health and fertility, and the ways in which their widespread use contributes to the culture of death at both the familial and societal levels. We ought to continue to advocate for policies and programs that support families, pregnant women, and adoption agencies, as well as those that improve foster care. We need to do better at a societal level, but we also need to do better as a Church. We need to have more patience and respect for the decisions of other people. There is no ideal family size; we need to stop criticizing families for having "too many" kids as well as scrutinizing couples' reasons for desiring to space births. These are decisions of conscience left to the prayerful discernment of the couple and ultimately to the will of the Author of life Himself.

Can we turn back the tide of our contraceptive culture? Is the solution to return to the legal prohibition of contraception? While there is much to be said for the instructive function of the law, we ought to concentrate our efforts where they will make the largest degree of difference: on a changing of hearts for a changing of society. Where possible, we ought to promote openness to life, interdependence on one another, and acceptance of weakness. Those of us who have children might do well to push the boundaries of social acceptability by including our children as much as possible — at church, in the grocery store, at restaurants, on airplanes.

This can be challenging and even humiliating, but if we want to contribute to a society that helps families flourish, we need to give others the opportunity to experience family life along with us. I have often been surprised and moved by the compassion of helpful strangers in our community, the consoling wisdom of grandmothers reminding me I will indeed miss these days, and the joy others take in the smiles and giggles of my little ones. While it can be tempting to let occasional harsh comments cloud our vision, we are called to be witnesses of Christ to the world. For those of us with children, this means being *in* the world *as a family* — with all the joy and messiness that family life entails.

CHAPTER 5

Unconditional Love Begins in the Womb

Congratulations, you're pregnant! The line has turned pink, and you've seen a tiny heartbeat flickering on the ultrasound machine. It is time to celebrate — isn't it? In the age of prenatal testing, we aren't so sure.

Since the legalization of abortion and the introduction of amniocentesis in the 1970s, genetic screenings and counseling have occupied increasingly prevalent roles in prenatal care. Prenatal testing gives parents insight into the genetic makeup of their growing baby in utero, allowing diagnoses of medical conditions of varying degrees of severity, from minor disability to life-limiting to fatal. Many (but by no means all) of these genetic conditions can be identified through simple, virtually risk-free blood tests in the first or second trimester. Receiving a diagnosis early in pregnancy allows parents time to process and to prepare for raising the affected child. While this is certainly a worthy end, the main practical function of prenatal testing is undeniably to determine whether to continue with or to abort the pregnancy. This is true both statistically and by the admission of genetic counselors and doctors alike.[1]

Because there are rarely in utero treatments for these genetic conditions, and no cures, prenatal testing is intended for the "prevention" of these conditions. As Barbara Katz Rothman points out in *The Tentative Pregnancy: How Amniocentesis Changes the Experience of Motherhood*, if there were no more abortion, "it is hard to envision the continued existence of legal prenatal diagnosis programs."[2] *Donum Vitae* is clear that, when used "for the purpose of eliminating foetuses which are affected by malformations or which are carriers of hereditary illness," prenatal testing is a "violation of the unborn child's right to life" and "an abuse of the … rights and duties of the spouses."[3]

Given this strong link to abortion, how are Catholics to regard prenatal genetic testing? If there are acceptable ways to use prenatal genetic tests, what are they? What ought to alarm us about their use, and what might we retain as life- and dignity-affirming? While *Donum Vitae* affirms that prenatal testing can be acceptable so long as it *"respects the life and integrity of the embryo and the human foetus and is directed towards its safeguarding or healing as an individual*,"[4] in practice it can be difficult to determine when, exactly, that is. With the purposes of screening obscured, the use of euphemistic language, and the failure to understand the pro-life position, the waters of prenatal testing can be muddy and difficult to navigate.

Deciding Whether to Screen

The challenge of wielding the powerful medical advances of our time is in using them well. How do we harness their power to create more hospitable, human societies? While prenatal tests such as amniocentesis carry with them a small risk of miscarriage (about 0.3 percent), the newest tests available depend only upon blood samples or measurements taken via ultrasound. This means that with virtually no risk to mother or baby, doctors can diagnose many conditions with "reasonable certainty" (which, as we will see later in this chapter, is a claim so dubious it borders on fraudulent). Among these conditions are Down syndrome (trisomy 21), Edwards syndrome (trisomy 18), Patau syndrome (trisomy 13), Tay-Sachs disease, sickle cell anemia, cystic fibrosis, and fragile X syndrome. Because there are no prenatal treatments available for these conditions, what the test results offer parents is information as well as time to adjust and prepare to meet the unique needs of their child. Parents of a child who receives a difficult prenatal diagnosis may find strength and peace in grieving lost expectations and preparing to face unexpected adversity. These technologies serve as important advances for families who bravely face these challenges, particularly in cases when the diagnosis is fatal or life-limiting. Prenatal diagnosis is acceptable whenever the information is obtained with proportionately little risk and used to affirm the dignity of and care for the growing child.

How do parents decide whether to screen? Especially for Catholic couples for whom abortion is off the table, the diagnostic powers of prenatal genetic tests may provide little relevant information. As the majority of these conditions will be diagnosed via ultrasound later in pregnancy, is there a problem with forgoing the early screenings altogether?

It is entirely acceptable to forgo prenatal genetic screenings and tests, and many parents find it freeing to prepare themselves to welcome their child in all his strengths and challenges, whatever they may be. Couples should discuss the risks and benefits of each test and make their decision together. Unfortunately, medical providers often do not disclose all of the risks of these tests, either because they view "risk" narrowly in medical terms, or because they are tragically unaware of some risks. For example, an additional benefit of forgoing screening is that it shelters families from eugenic and economic pressures from doctors and insurance companies. This was the case for a Louisiana couple whose first child had cystic fibrosis. When their second child's screening came back positive for cystic fibrosis, their Health Maintenance Organization [HMO] threatened to withdraw coverage for both the new baby and the older brother if they didn't abort.[5] In this case, the HMO ultimately reversed its decision when threatened with a lawsuit, but denial of care is a regular occurrence.[6] For parents who refuse to consider abortion and are prepared to accept their children under any and all circumstances, opting out of these tests may lead to a less stressful pregnancy.

In addition to being less stressful, it may also be life-saving. One 2016 study showed that the number one factor determining whether newborns with life-limiting genetic diagnoses would survive to be discharged was the timing of the diagnosis.[7] Of the infants who were diagnosed after birth, only 1 percent died in the first 24 hours, and 87 percent lived to be sent home with their families. [8] For those who were diagnosed prenatally, outcomes were much grimmer: 36 percent died in the first 24 hours, and only 47 percent survived to be discharged.[9] The most likely explanation for these statistics is that, unfortunately, the expectation of negative outcomes, primarily on the part of providers who are aware of genetic prenatal diagnoses, can become a self-fulfilling prophecy. Providers who are taught that life-limiting diagnoses are inevitably fatal do not provide the same standard of care to these newborns as they do for newborns without genetic diagnoses. Instead of receiving whatever standard treatments might be offered, these babies are given "comfort care" with the expectation that their lives will be incredibly short. And when treatments are limited in this manner, their lives *are* incredibly short. Given the minimal benefit of prenatal genetic screenings, the risk for denial of coverage, and the limited care for infants who are given these diagnoses prenatally, it is no wonder that many families choose to forgo these types of screenings entirely.

On the other hand, knowledge is power, or so the saying goes. Even for parents who intend to keep their baby regardless of diagnosis, the benefit of time and preparation for the unique needs indicated by these diagnoses may outweigh any potential resistance from doctors or struggles with insurance coverage.

One option might be to consider the degree of genetic risk for the couple involved and limit testing to only those conditions for which there might be a high degree of likelihood. Tay-Sachs, for example, disproportionately affects those of Jewish ancestry, while the primary risk factor for Down syndrome is increased maternal age, beginning around age thirty-five and increasing from there. Early testing with negative results might allay fears and anxieties, making the time of pregnancy a more pleasant space for preparation. Another option is for parents to undergo pre-pregnancy carrier screening themselves to identify conditions for which their children might be at risk. This, too, can give parents peace by quantifying the degree of risk for their growing baby of various health conditions.

The decision to screen or not is personal and will depend on a variety of factors, ranging from the parents' own medical conditions and family history to the perceived burdens and benefits of the respective screenings. There is ample justification for the decision to forgo all screenings as well as to embrace every possible option. Either end of the spectrum and everything in between is entirely licit, so long as the information obtained serves to further the dignity of the child to be born.

The Abortive Mentality and Eugenic Trends

While none of these screening options are illicit in themselves, they have been used for devastating ends. Any intention to use the information, however licitly obtained, for the destruction of the unborn person is gravely evil. While most parents undergo screening with no plan to abort on the basis of the results, 80 percent decide to abort in the face of severe congenital abnormality.[10] In Denmark, where all pregnancies are routinely screened for Down syndrome regardless of maternal age, 95 percent of those positively diagnosed are aborted.[11]

Perhaps one of the more tragic implications of the abortive mentality detailed in chapter 4 has been this impulse to stamp out disability. As emerging technology allows us access to data about the being growing within us, the use of that information as justification for abortion at the individual level has resulted in a large-scale eugenic extermination. For example, 90 to 95 percent of babies diagnosed with Down syndrome are aborted, resulting in the near elimination of the next generation of people with Down syndrome in countries like Denmark and Iceland.[12] It may not be a systematic effort by the state, but the numbers add up. As hearts and wombs close to people affected by these conditions, they are slowly disappearing altogether.

The drive for prenatal testing that can be carried out

at increasingly early gestational ages is tied directly to the timeline of abortion, medically, and arguably emotionally, less complicated in the earlier weeks of pregnancy. While amniocentesis has been used since the early 1970s, it carries a small risk of miscarriage and is usually performed at eighteen weeks. Abortion after this age is painful to the fetus, involving dismemberment and removal of its body. Diagnosing genetic conditions earlier means that the mother has had less time to bond with her growing baby. Chorionic villus sampling (CVS) involves testing the placental tissue, and while it can be done as early as ten weeks, it carries a 1 percent risk of miscarriage, higher than that for amniocentesis. The blood tests currently available detect placental DNA in the mother's blood as early as nine weeks, making for a lower-risk test at a stage when the fetus is small enough that abortion can be done via suction.

The abortive mentality leads to a phenomenon of conditional pregnancy, what Barbara Katz Rothman termed "the tentative pregnancy" in her 1986 exploration of the then-emerging technology of amniocentesis.[13] As one of the earliest instantiations of contemporary prenatal testing, amniocentesis sought to identify abnormal traits for treatment, to prepare parents, or, most troublingly, to eliminate defective children prior to their birth through abortion. Before amniocentesis and ultrasound, parents rarely had an idea of the particulars of the baby in the womb.

The phenomenon of a tentative pregnancy — the idea

that continuing pregnancy is in any way dependent upon the "quality" of the human being undergoing gestation — is entirely repugnant to the Christian ethos. As difficult as it is, we must grapple with this dark side of reproductive technologies and fight on behalf of the weakest among us: those who are unborn and those who live with disability. We must continue legal and social battles to protect the disabled and to provide better services to assist them and their families toward greater human flourishing.

The abortive mentality (abortion as a failsafe for contraception) and an intolerance for imperfection create increased pressure to eliminate those who are disabled. Abortion of the disabled might be sold as "freedom" to allow parents to escape from the additional burden and suffering that caring for disabled children necessarily entails, but what of the freedom of these children to exist? Is there a threshold for minimal functioning at which we deserve to exist? For that matter, what is the threshold of "acceptable" burden and suffering in parenthood? The reality is that all parents expect and undergo a degree of imposition when caring for their children. Children are inconvenient, expensive, noisy, needy, messy, and vexing; as *any* parent will tell you, parenthood is not for the faint of heart (or the weak of stomach).

An abortive mentality that treats pregnancy as conditional upon the perceived likely quality of the child in utero is not compatible with the task of parenthood. Like marriage, parenthood is a sacred covenant, including the acceptance of the unknown — more so, really, in that you cannot know anything of the child you hope to welcome. Parenthood is truly Godlike in its attempt to welcome, embrace, and love the other fully and unconditionally. Placing conditions on that which, despite our best efforts, remains beyond our control serves as poor preparation indeed for parenthood. The more we attempt control, the more we treat our progeny as products, the more likely we are to demean those we deem defective. A faith-filled posture (the only logical posture as we attempt this leap into the unknown) is our only authentic choice if we wish to receive the responsibility of stewardship of the immortal soul God places in our care. This is far from regarding children as objects to be obtained for the satisfaction of parental desires.

Increasing pressure to abort "defective" fetuses results in decreasing populations of people who are affected by genetic conditions, which in turn triggers a decrease in resources for these populations. As abortion (and eventually euthanasia) becomes a "panacea" for dealing with these diagnoses and these populations shrink, arguments against allocating resources to promote the dignity and flourishing of these populations gain strength, at least from a utilitarian perspective. Prenatal diagnosis is compatible with a culture of life only when it is deployed *in service to* these individuals, their families, and communities of support. To the extent that it detracts from their chances at life, the services available to them, and their opportunities for community with other individuals who are like them, it can be categorized as violent and malicious.

Unreliable Tests

A further tragedy is that these tests are, in many cases, subject to a large degree of error. Despite their being touted as 99 percent accurate, an investigation of four of the major diagnostic blood tests revealed their accuracy to be about 50 percent.[14] In the case of trisomy 13, the American College of Obstetricians and Gynecologists estimates that a positive result is correct only 9 percent of the time.[15] Despite this overwhelming degree of inaccuracy, 63 percent of physicians believe that abortion is a justifiable response to genetic anomalies, and that number jumps to 90 percent for life-limiting conditions like trisomy 13.[16] With no approval for their use required by the FDA, there is little to hold the companies that produce these tests accountable for the faulty information that has, in all mathematical likelihood, led to many abortions of healthy, unaffected babies.

When my younger brother tested positive for spina bifida at sixteen weeks, my mother refused to discuss the abortion suggested by the doctor. At his birth, it was immediately clear that he did not have the disorder. As a teen, he took third place at the Junior National Air Rifle championship and today enjoys near perfect health, scaling mountains and climbing boulders in his free time. This is not to argue that my brother somehow deserved to live more than someone who truly was affected by spina bifida. On the contrary, it is entirely possible that someone born with spina bifida might be an altogether more worthy human being than my brother in spite of (or perhaps because of) the difficulties he must face. The point is that women (and their partners) have been influenced to do violence to their unborn children on the basis of tests that are no more predictive than a coin flip. It is unconscionable to consider administering these early, inaccurate tests as acceptable medical practice on the basis that their results make the decision to abort easier.

Difficult Cases

Some children receive diagnoses that are significantly challenging, both from the perspective of faith and from the requirements for their basic care. It is hard to grapple with the idea that God would allow our children to be affected by life-limiting and fatal diagnoses. Children with trisomy 13, for example, are affected by severe physical deformities and heart conditions, and seldom live past the first year of life. The care demanded by their special needs is intense. The chance of a baby diagnosed with trisomy 13 living past the first year of life is less than 10 percent (although those who do survive the first year have an 80 percent chance of living until age five).[17]

There is no doubt that the care for these infants is demanding, or that the loss felt by their parents is immense. And yet the demands are not so different from those placed on families called to care for a loved one who suffers a severe head injury, or a spouse rendered dependent due to dementia or Alzheimer's. To dare to love is risky and demanding; that these demands make themselves known earlier or in unexpected ways does not lessen the responsibilities we have to our children to care for them, to love them, and to welcome them with open arms regardless of any limitations they may have.

Compounding the issue in these cases of life-limiting fatal diagnoses is a glaring lack of informed consent. Doctors themselves often receive medical training that omits any treatment options in these cases aside from abortion. Because they are taught that *the* "treatment" for fatal diagnosis is abortion and carry that notion into their practice, their experience of any other response is severely limited. They lack the knowledge and experience to inform parents of other options.

But there *are* other options, and increasingly, families who receive these kinds of diagnoses are able to find one another. They might connect via social media or receive support from organizations such as Be Not Afraid, a nonprofit that supports families who receive a prenatal diagnosis and carry the child to term. Studies have shown that when US parents are offered perinatal hospice support, they choose to carry their babies to term 75 to 85 percent of the time.[18] This is most certainly a blessing, not only for the babies who are given a chance at life they otherwise might not have, but for mothers and their families. Research overwhelmingly demonstrates that the choice to keep their babies, no matter how dire the diagnosis, is one that mothers not only do not regret, but feel immensely positive about.[19] The studies do not report similarly positive outcomes for women who choose abortion. In contrast to the joy and gratitude expressed by 97 percent of the

women who chose to keep their babies after lethal diagnoses, women who chose abortion reported significantly
more despair and depression.[20]

Our call as Christians is to lift up these voices and
share their stories. We must be witnesses to the fundamental truth that applies to us all: Our flaws and struggles do not and cannot disqualify us from life. Suffering
is real and it is hard, but the way to face it is not to hang
our heads in despair. We know from Christ's witness on
the cross that suffering does not have the last word; love
does. Flaws, weaknesses, and vulnerabilities are common
to us all, and it does none of us good to decide which we
are unwilling to tolerate. It is not by refusing to suffer that
we find more joy, become more human, or make life more
bearable. It is by patiently walking shoulder to shoulder,
each of us accompanying the other, each of us making up
for something the other lacks, each of us witnessing to the
inextinguishable power of the human spirit.

Unconditional Love, Unconditional Pregnancy

Can screening technology ever be understood separately
from the abortive mentality? However dark some applications of this technology can be, the answer is yes. When
used appropriately, prenatal testing can aid families by
offering parents time to prepare practically, socially, and
emotionally for the particular and unexpected needs that
may arise with certain diagnoses. Learning to let go of
preconceived notions and accept the child before you is

the challenge of every parent; with some diagnoses, this challenge comes sooner and can be greater in magnitude. Prenatal screening offers parents the opportunity to grieve a once-imagined future and prepare to welcome the child God has entrusted to them with openness and joy.

It is, of course, a completely legitimate choice to forgo any and all screenings. Some parents might feel liberated by a pregnancy that is less medicalized, free from agonizing over test results. Opting out may help to facilitate a spiritual posture of acceptance. Depending on the nature of the conditions in question, this may apply even to those who are aware of heightened risks of genetic abnormalities. While some advanced preparations may be particularly helpful for conditions in which serious interventions are warranted, many conditions are such that advance knowledge would not significantly improve the outcome. In these cases, the approach to prenatal testing should depend on the preferences and temperaments of the parents. Regarding additional tests and preparations, what causes anxiety to rise in one mother might quell the fears of another.

Regardless of our personal convictions, the medical community within which the majority of us in the developed world receive our care operates out of the assumption that all embryos are inherently *un*equal, their value depending upon a myriad of factors: whether their existence was intended or desired, the method of their conception, their gender, and their genetic makeup. The perceived value of an embryo is an amalgamation of whatever lies in the eyes of its beholders. Embryos' fates are inherently uncertain; even those who are intentionally brought into being within a laboratory setting are subject to intense scrutiny; many are discarded, some are frozen, few make it out alive (see chapters 9 and 10 for more on IVF, gamete donation, and surrogacy). We regard the days of deformed children being dashed on the rocks in ancient Rome with horror, and yet today our actions and intent are very similar. We are removed from the action, and our victims are younger, it's true, but the result is the same. Those deemed unfit for life are stamped out at the earliest opportunity.

When we treat pregnancy as conditional, we fail to embody our feminine genius. There is no in-between — there is the time before this new life existed, and there is the time afterward. Our bodies mediate the relationship between this tiny life and the rest of the world, but the demands upon us to welcome and nurture are immediate. We must be witnesses to the fact that struggles and flaws, no matter the degree, do not disqualify human beings from life; and under no circumstances may we allow suffering to have the last word.

CHAPTER 6

This Is My Body, Given Up for You: Childbirth and the Paschal Mystery

Perhaps the most profound way in which woman uniquely images her Creator is in her capacity to bring forth new life. Reaching so deeply into her identity, it is not surprising that the choices surrounding childbirth are perhaps some of the most personal a woman can make, as they regard one of the most intimate experiences of her life. Yet so often these "choices" are dictated by medical circumstances (or so she is told) or made for her by medical providers who are in some cases complete strangers to her, determined by the lottery of an on-call schedule. The timing of spontaneous labor is nearly impossible to control, and the likelihood that a woman's physician of choice will be available to deliver is often no better than chance. And paradoxically, as labor and birth in our culture have moved over the last century from the home to the hospital, their association with pain and fear have grown. Recognizing that God designed women with the capacity for childbirth, how can we move away from fear and toward greater trust in the plan He has written into our bodies?

While the medical techniques popularized in the last century have certainly made *some* births — true emergencies — safer for women, much of this "safety" has come at the sacrifice of women's own consent and participation in childbirth. Additionally, although interventions such as induction and cesarean section (C-section) can be lifesaving under certain conditions, they often lead to unnecessary complications in births that are more medically straightforward. Women who give birth in the United States do so in the "most dangerous place in the developed world to give birth," with maternal mortality rates currently at 0.02 percent *and rising,* rather than decreasing over time.[1] Fear of birth, rather than trust in our own bodies, is the prevailing sentiment, and even mothers whose birth experiences result in healthy outcomes for mother and baby report traumatic childbirth experiences at the hands of healthcare providers.[2] Women's voices in their own care are routinely dismissed, at times callously, by "experts" who assert control and demean the women who either question the status quo or have the audacity to voice their preferences for birthing options.

If we want to improve birth outcomes and make the delivery room a truly life- and dignity-affirming space for every woman, then we need to start taking a hard look at our assumptions and practices surrounding childbirth. What is the average experience of birth like for women in America, and how did it come to be this way? What do researchers and women themselves have to say about how to make birth experiences safer and more positive? What can we do to rewrite our cultural birth narratives to more closely reflect the truth of what is good for laboring women and empower women to advocate for themselves and their unborn children in the delivery room?

Childbirth Throughout History

For much of the history of the world, childbirth belonged in the hands of women. In many indigenous cultures, it still does. Midwives and other female family and community members attended labor and birth, passing down knowledge and techniques for pain reduction, optimal birthing positions, and herbal treatments to the next generation. While advances in medicine and technology have certainly been powerful, not all shifts in the process of childbirth have benefited women. As this natural process moved from bedrooms to hospitals, becoming increasingly medicalized, what was once a realm of female power and expertise has been wrested from women's hands and placed in those of physicians. Many contemporary "advances" have come at the cost of depersonalizing and dehumanizing the treatment of laboring women.

With the invention of forceps in the early seventeenth century, surgeons (men) began attending births and often rushing labor by premature use of the forceps, sometimes even before full dilation. By the 1920s, it was something of standard practice to deliver babies via forceps and a large episiotomy. This is the invention that popularized the back-lying lithotomy position of birth that has now become the norm. Despite making the process lengthier and more difficult for the laboring mother by working against the flow of gravity and narrowing the pelvic outlet, this position makes it easiest for medical professionals to employ various birthing instruments. Beginning around 1910, early feminists began to advocate for escape from the pains of childbirth via the use of medications, such as chloroform, and through the 1950s, use of Twilight Sleep, a mixture of narcotic and amnesiac medication, became popular.[3] Although they gave birth screaming and often were tied down or straight-jacketed, women remembered essentially nothing of the experience, save the occasional horrific flashback.[4]

With the development of the Friedman curve in 1955 as a standardized measure of progression of labor came the technomedical model of birth we know today. As Leah Jacobson reflects, "All of these practices were meant to make birth safer, quicker, and less painful, but some may have resulted in robbing women of the experience altogether and left them wondering about their own abilities to naturally birth their children."[5] This lack of confidence in our bodies' natural abilities has grown deep roots and, particularly in the United States, led to an overemphasis on medicalized childbirth that, despite challenges, continues today.

This method of childbirth, with doctors and nurses the primary agents and women mentally absent, was standard for over fifty years before it began to be challenged by doctors, feminists, and midwives who envisioned a better way. The 1960s and 1970s saw increased emphasis on the importance of midwifery and working with a woman's body to facilitate childbirth naturally. Midwife Ina May Gaskin and her husband founded a commune known as "The Farm" in Tennessee as a midwifery center. In over two thousand births on The Farm from 1970 to 2010, the home birthrate was nearly 95 percent, with a cesarean rate of 1.7 percent and a maternal mortality rate of 0.[6] Despite statistics that point to the positive outcomes of midwife and home birth, the standard of care in the United States remains the obstetric model.

Midwifery versus the Technomedical Model

The practice of midwifery has long been — however falsely — identified with witchcraft, and something of a witch hunt continues today. However dismal our childbirth outcomes have become, we still suffer from a prejudice that privileges the scientific over the natural. Women who have birth plans are sometimes openly mocked, stereotyped as "crunchy," high-maintenance, and out of touch with the realities of birth. Even some feminists are harshly critical of the notion that minimizing interventions, including the use of epidural and pain medications, might in some way benefit women. "No one ever asks a man if he's having a 'natural root canal.' No one ever asks a man if he is having a 'natural vasectomy,'" Jessi Klein points out.[7] This might be a fair criticism if childbirth were indeed the extraction of something diseased, the pain a sign that something has gone wrong. But labor contractions are part of the physiological process in its ideal, signaling that everything is going right. Research suggests that the very intensity of the contractions that we seek to dull contributes to vital bonding processes.[8] For all that we claim to be a society devoted to science, we appear to be very suspicious of research surrounding the natural process of childbirth.

Take, for example, the two midwifery centers in the UK analyzed by author Milli Hill in her book *Give Birth Like a Feminist*. One-to-One Midwives and the Albany Midwifery Practice both have outstanding credentials. One-to-One's home birthrate is 97 percent, and their still-birth rate and neonatal death rates are a half and a quarter of the UK average, respectively. Albany beat the UK's average stats by leaps and bounds as well, with a 20 percent lower induction rate, 10 percent lower C-section rate, and only 30 percent of mothers experiencing any vaginal tearing (and with no fourth-degree tears at all). The UK's Royal College of Obstetrics and Gynecology states that 90 percent of women will tear during birth. Despite overwhelmingly positive outcomes, both practices faced intense scrutiny, and Albany was suddenly shut down by the King's College Trust due to "safety concerns" with no evidence offered as to the reasoning behind the decision. Sadly, despite all the evidence that midwifery care is a great deal more effective than hospital birth by many measures, these modern manifestations mirror the witch hunts for the midwives of the Middle Ages. Whether this hunt is couched as surveillance, persecution, or merely regulation, Hill observes, "Those who believe that maternity safety will only be achieved by technocracy and the absolute dominance of obstetrics will certainly not feel that there is anything wrong with pulling into line [anyone who] misguidedly thinks there is a value to 'hands off,' 'physiological,' or even 'normal' birth."[9]

This perspective of the physician as the primary mediator of childbirth dominates our view in the United States as well. A former coworker of mine scoffed at my suggestions about learning breathing techniques, informing me that she intended to get the epidural and that her physician had instructed her, "Leave that to me. I will coach you through." Her epidural worked only on one side, and despite his lofty promises, the physician was not present for the birth. My sister-in-law eyed me with suspicion as I cited statistics among my reasons for forgoing interventions at my hospital birth. "I'll still probably get the epidural," she responded. Despite being both a nurse and one of the strongest women I know, when it came to birthing her baby, she lacked confidence in her own abilities. And though the statistics on positive outcomes for women who forgo interventions are available for those willing to entertain the idea, more often the assumption of women is that they "could never do" what so many generations of mothers have done before them.

How have we ended up with a birth culture so steeped in fear that women are reluctant even to discuss their options among friends, preferring to leave all in the hands of the establishment? Why are we so quick to doubt the ability of our own bodies to do as they were designed to do, so ready to mock women who opt out of a medical setting that is, by all statistics, *not* as safe as we believe it to be?

Choices in Childbirth

One of the unintended results of medicalizing childbirth is that women's knowledge of their own bodies and their own capabilities is much more limited than it has been historically (and still is in indigenous cultures), when helping with the childbirth of a close family member or neighbor went much deeper than dropping off a hot casserole. Women commonly filled the role of doula if not midwife for one another. Today, the first childbirth a woman experiences is often her own. The most trusted expert she may rely on is her doctor. In many cases, this means an OB, a physician whose specialty is obstetric surgery. And while these physicians have intensive training in the aspects of and techniques for when the process goes wrong, few are ever formally trained to facilitate or have even witnessed natural, unmedicated childbirth.[10] They see the process of childbirth primarily through the lens of medical ailment.

In the United States, this has led to a birth culture in which women surrender more of their power and autonomy in the process of birth than they otherwise might. We mentally place childbirth in the same category as kidney removal, when in reality these are substantially different processes. An overly medicalized approach to childbirth contributes to rates of induction, C-section, and maternal mortality that are significantly higher than those of other developed countries.[11] One of the primary differences between the United States and many other developed countries is the type of health care practitioner who normally oversees prenatal care and childbirth. When we privilege obstetric care over midwife care, we privilege the surgical over the natural. As a country, we have medicalized a natural process when, in the majority of cases, a natural approach is in the better interest of mother and baby.[12]

This is not to say that a blanket approach suffices for all women or indeed all pregnancies. The argument here is that expectant mothers don't have the information they need to make truly informed choices. While the gap is lessening in the age of social media, blogs, and YouTube, it ought not to be only the women who seek out information about childbirth who benefit. All pregnant women have the right to greater education and transparency than it is currently the standard practice to provide. Women need to be informed and empowered to make as many decisions regarding prenatal care and childbirth as are medically safe for the pregnancy in question.

The choices in childbirth ought not to be presented as mere preferences, nor should they be made out of fear. Often, the "choice" of C-section or vaginal delivery, for example, is made by the circumstances of the particular pregnancy as they present themselves, but not always. Women should not be in a position where their choice for an epidural is motivated primarily by fear of pain, or where they are given Pitocin because an OB has a dinner engagement. We owe women more than that. If an expectant mother follows the recommended guidelines for prenatal care, she attends ten or more appointments. That should be ample time to discuss childbirth options and labor interventions so that women can make informed decisions about childbirth based on the expertise and recommendations of their providers. Instead, most women who come by this information do so on their own time, informing themselves through reading and opting in to childbirth classes.

These usually well-educated, usually white women are often mocked for having the audacity to form opinions about how they would like to give birth, to the point of being referred to as "birthzillas" by the very providers they turn to for assistance.[13] And yet the disparity between outcomes for white mothers and those for their minority counterparts is shocking. According to the CDC, most pregnancy-related deaths are preventable, and maternal mortality rates are two to three times higher for Black and Native women.[14] If we want to reverse these statistics and change the tide for all women, but especially for those most at risk, perhaps we ought to be *promoting* education about choices in childbirth rather than leaving women in the hands of a system that is structured for intervention and efficiency over personalized care.

In *The Business of Being Born*, documentary filmmakers Ricki Lake and Abby Epstein detail what they call the "cascade of interventions." When a woman in labor reports to the hospital, she is summarily placed within an existing structure of hospital policies regarding timing and progression of labor. These policies are developed with an eye toward both safety and efficiency, dictating when and how women must be monitored and their labor sped up according to established timelines. There are rules to govern everything, from induction to administration of pain medications and epidurals. The intricate web of childbirth interventions earns the name "cascade of interventions" because these interventions are so enmeshed with each other. Whether by medical necessity or hospital policies, having any of these interventions increases the likelihood of needing another. Women who are induced via the drug Pitocin, for example, experience contractions that are much stronger than they might be naturally. Often their intensity is such that women turn to the epidural to escape. Epidurals can slow labor, and so more Pitocin is given to again increase the intensity of the contractions. Women who have epidurals cannot move around as freely, and so are more likely to give birth on their backs in the lithotomy position. Because this position is suboptimal for movement of the baby through the pelvis, it is more likely that doctors will need to cut episiotomies, or to use vacuum or forceps. Epidurals can also cause fever for both mother and baby, and the unnaturally strong contractions can cause heart decelerations for the baby, all of which increase the likelihood that attempts at vaginal delivery will be abandoned in favor of C-section, statistically riskier for both mother and baby. [15]

On the other hand, we have the option of forgoing these types of interventions and trusting our bodies to do that natural work of labor that God has made them to do. Author of *Give Birth Like a Feminist* Milli Hill explains:

> The argument against being anesthetized is that not only will you miss out on the human experience [of birth] itself, but that the drugs themselves may bring other problems, such as side effects for you and the baby, interference with the production of your own labor hormones, a higher chance of intervention, difficulties with bonding or breastfeeding, and negative long-term effects from the interventions themselves, for example pelvic floor issues … or nerve damage caused by epidural.[16]

The alternative is what Ina May Gaskin terms "clean" labor pain, leaning into the natural processes of labor in which the pain ceases with the cessation of labor: "When avoidance of pain becomes the major emphasis of childbirth care, the paradoxical effect is that more women have to deal with pain *after* their babies are born."[17] Relying on the natural progression of labor to move the baby through the birth canal and relying on social support from husbands, midwives, doulas, and family members reduces the need for interventions and pain relief alike, and contributes to a faster recovery following birth.

Natural or home birth is not appropriate in every case, and we have much to be grateful for in the way of birthing advancements. Especially for conditions like preeclampsia and other medical emergencies, the obstetric model is life-saving. But must it be all or nothing? When we look at the trajectory of medicalized birth, circumstances are brighter today than in the days when women were drugged, blindfolded, and strapped to a table. Still, the drive toward the humanization of birth is far from over. We need to promote conversations about options and create opportunities for physicians to learn from midwives and doulas and to attend home births as part of their education. Whatever our rhetoric, a healthy baby is not *all* that matters! We can work to minimize birth trauma and promote education so fewer women have birth stories that smack of Stephen King and even fewer are left lamenting, "If only I had known ..."

Embracing the Paschal Mystery of Birth
Historically, some have insisted that the pain of labor stems from God's just judgment of Adam and Eve in the book of Genesis: "I will greatly increase your pangs in childbearing; in pain you shall bring forth children" (3:16).

From this perspective, the pain of childbirth is another of God's punishments of humanity, a consequence of original sin. There are those who argue that this punishment is not something we should seek to ameliorate: Women should willingly submit to the pain of labor and not look for escape.

That view has been widely criticized as misogynistic and, indeed, seems to clash with the ethos of Christianity many of us experience today. Still, the pain and suffering of labor are realities to which we as Christians ought to pay attention. To minimize pain and suffering is a laudable goal of medicine. In the case of labor and birth, however, it may not always be the most vital. Central to our faith is not the escape from suffering, but the transformation of it. As Catholics, we understand that, through prayer, we can join our own sufferings to those of Jesus on the cross and, in doing so, participate in the work of salvation.

This is how we offer up our sufferings, and so, too, we can prayerfully offer up the suffering we face in childbirth. Regardless of method or circumstance, all birthing mothers are invited into the Paschal Mystery — that is, the redemptive power of the suffering, death, and resurrection of Jesus — in a very real, tangible way. Kimberly Hahn connects the Paschal Mystery to childbirth: "The labor and delivery of our child is a 'paschal sign,' which mirrors Christ's self-offering and resurrection. We offer our lives so that our child may live now and live forever."[18] The image of childbirth as paschal sign comes from Pope St. John Paul II's *Letter to Families*, where he points out that this imagery originates with Christ himself in the Gospel of John: "The 'hour' of Christ's death is compared here to the 'hour' of the woman in birthpangs; the birth of a new child fully reflects the victory of life over death brought about by the Lord's Resurrection."[19] In the process of birth, mothers join with Christ crucified and through their suffering bring forth new life. With every contraction, a mother can pray along with her Savior: "This is my body, which is given for you" (Lk 22:19).

Learning from Mary's Posture of Surrender

Another Christian approach to childbirth fittingly looks to Mary, Mother of God. The idea that Mary was preserved from the pains of childbirth has long been a part of the tradition of the Church. As the immaculately conceived Mother of God, Mary was without original sin and so exempt from the consequence of sin, which makes it reasonable to believe that she was not subject to painful childbirth. This view, although not proclaimed infallibly, has been articulated by popes and Church Fathers, and even appears in the Catechism of the Council of Trent.[20] Others might argue that freedom from the pain of childbirth does not necessarily follow from Mary's immaculate conception. Despite being preserved from original sin and its effects within her own soul, Mary clearly did experience the consequences of original sin — at least those that follow from existing in a world full of its effects. Mary suffers alongside her son at His Passion, a sword "pierce[s]" her heart as Simeon most poignantly predicted in Luke

2:35. Why should she be preserved from pain during childbirth, specifically, when suffering is clearly a part of God's future plans for His Son and His mother?

The view that Mary was mystically preserved from the pain of childbirth rests on the assumption that these pains are in fact God's punishment to humanity, an intentional punitive act on God's part applying only to women. This is not the only way to understand the Genesis text, however. The consequences of an act are not always externally imposed, as is a punishment exercised by an authority figure. Some consequences are intrinsic to an act; one cannot commit the act without also thereby bringing about a consequence. I cannot jump off a bridge without falling. If I jump off that bridge and hit the concrete, my death is not an imposed punishment, but an intrinsic consequence of my poor choice to jump. Viewing the pains of childbirth as an intrinsic consequence of the Fall can help us reconcile feminist objections to this supposed punishment with how Mary was able to avoid experiencing that consequence by virtue of her sinlessness.

For we now know that childbirth is not intrinsically painful. Many women experience painless and even pleasurable births; there is even some evidence that it is possible to experience orgasm during this process![21] As we have seen, research indicates that fear contributes to the experience of pain during childbirth, in what has been termed the fear-tension-pain cycle.[22] Movements such as hypnobirthing, home birth, and the Positive Birth Movement have cropped up in response to this research, seeking to empower and support women to have more affirming, less painful birth experiences. Much of the focus is on removing fear from the birthing experience. Hypnobirthing classes, for example, instruct women to think of their contractions as "surges," to welcome these physical waves as part of the natural birthing process rather than viewing them as pains to endure.

Women who experience childbirth with this humanistic or midwifery model of care report much more positively about their birth experiences than do their standard techno-medical counterparts, citing greater satisfaction and less anxiety.[23] They are also less likely to lose their babies and less likely to experience preterm birth.[24] Given what we know about birth scientifically and psychologically, it is possible to understand Mary's painless experience of childbirth as the perfect birth, one unmarred by fear and steeped in trust in the Lord's plan for our bodies.

We could continue to debate whether Mary felt pain in childbirth, but better questions might be: "What can we learn from Mary's approach to childbirth?" And "How does what we know about the way God made our bodies complement that approach?" We were made to bear life, a fact better suited to the new birthing paradigm that is taking hold: one that views birth as a natural process, rather than viewing all births primarily through the lens of what can go wrong. Just as we have been taught to suppress our fertility as a problem in need of correction, so too we have been taught to fear childbirth (or turn it into something to be feared). Learning from Mary's perfect acceptance of the Father's will can help us trade our fear for trust in His loving plan. Mary loved God purely and perfectly, and as Saint John tells us, "Perfect love casts out fear," (1 Jn 4:18). The more deeply we grow in love and trust, the less fear can take hold. Letting go of pain in childbirth may be as simple (though not easy) as learning to surrender alongside Mary.

CHAPTER 7

My Flesh Is True Food: The Spiritual and Physical Nourishment of Nursing

The physical gift of self inherent to motherhood doesn't stop with pregnancy and childbirth. Every nursing mother can say along with Jesus, "Take, eat; this is my body" (Mt 26:26). Like pregnancy and childbirth, the act of nourishing an infant with one's body is as deeply intimate as it is physically demanding.

While the physical, emotional, financial, and even spiritual benefits of breastfeeding are well documented, only a small fraction of American mothers breastfeed for the duration recommended by health experts. The American Academy of Pediatrics (AAP) recommends that children be breastfed through the first year, and the WHO the first two years, with breastfeeding being their exclusive source of nutrition for the first six months. Of the 80 percent of American mothers who initiate breastfeeding, only 22.3 percent are still exclusively breastfeeding at the minimum recommendation of six months.[1] That number is even smaller for Latina and Black populations. Why is it that, despite overwhelming benefits of exclusive breastfeeding, so few American babies have been able to receive those benefits in recent years? What are the factors that limit breastfeeding in the US, and how can we work to address them to ensure that a greater number of women and children can experience these free and natural benefits?

Misconceptions about Ability to Breastfeed

Some of these low statistics may be due to the misconception that a significant number of women are medically unable to breastfeed. Women who believe this to be true are less likely to persevere through obstacles to breastfeeding than women who understand that this population constitutes a small minority. Because the medical facts are so widely misunderstood, it bears some argument to articulate just how *un*common a medical inability to breastfeed really is. Five percent is commonly cited as the percentage of mothers who are medically unable to breastfeed. Research by La Leche League International reveals that this incidence is not supported by recent studies but has its origins in the opening lecture at the 1938 Annual Meeting of the British Medical Association.[2]

While there is a lack of research to pinpoint an exact number, current estimates are much lower, around 0.1 percent or 1 in 1,000 women.[3] If this estimate is correct, 99.9 percent of women are physically able to produce enough milk to feed their babies, though there are additional medical reasons for women to forgo breastfeeding. The WHO lists few medical reasons that preclude breastfeeding, including untreated HIV infection where there is access to safe water, sepsis, untreated herpes type 1 virus, and use of certain medications (sedating psychotherapeutic drugs, anti-epileptic drugs and opioids, radioactive iodine-131, topical iodine, and cytotoxic chemotherapy).[4] If we include women whose medical conditions contraindicate breastfeeding (even when it is physically possible), the percentage of women "medically unable" to breastfeed increases, but given the rarity of the circumstances listed by the WHO, that increase is not much.

Still, ruling out medical difficulties with breastfeeding does nothing to address the myriad of other obstacles mothers may encounter. The purpose of laying out these statistics is to establish that many more American women can breastfeed than those who believe that they can, and naturally the belief that something is *possible* is fundamental in supporting one's efforts to persevere through obstacles that may arise. Among these obstacles are lack of partner support, lack of paid maternity leave, and lack of workplace accommodations for pumping requirements. Due to the supply-demand relationship of feeding and breast milk supply, it is far more common for women to face secondary breastfeeding insufficiency — in which lack of knowledge or support hampers mothers' efforts to initiate breastfeeding, resulting in suboptimal supply — than it is for women to be medically unable to produce breast milk. Even women who can physically breastfeed may choose to forgo that option due to the burden of these additional factors, especially given the widespread availability of cleverly marketed formulas.

Fed or Breast — Which Is Best?

In recent years, research comparing breast milk with artificial formula has yielded mountains of evidence in support of the superiority of the "real deal." The "Breast Is Best" public health campaign began in the 1990s as a WHO effort to support women and increase the number of mothers who initiate and sustain breastfeeding through the first six months. As a result of this growing awareness of the advantages of breastfeeding, hospitals now vie for the coveted designation of "Baby-Friendly" according to WHO-UNICEF guidelines.[5] Hospitals garner the Baby-Friendly hospital designation by adopting policies such as "rooming in" (newborns stay with their mothers rather than in nurseries), observance of the "golden hour" just following birth (in which baths and exams come *after* mom and baby have their first moments of bonding), avoidance of formula feeding, and availability of on-staff lactation consultants to help new mothers establish breast-feeding. Baby-Friendly hospitals often have large posters of babies nuzzling at their mother's chests, with large lettering declaring, "Breast is best!"

Given the large disparity between the number of women who initiate breastfeeding and those who continue to do so through six months, it should not be surprising that a movement has arisen to counter the "Breast Is Best" campaign. The "Fed Is Best" movement seeks to combat formula-feeding mothers' feelings of shame and inadequacy over their perceived failure to choose the optimal feeding method for their children. It ought to go without saying that feeding their children is a top priority for mothers, and it is true that, in a limited number of circumstances, women may face medical challenges that entirely preclude the possibility of breastfeeding. More often, though, the challenges that women face are of a different nature: social, economic, or emotional limits that are seemingly insurmountable.

A single mother with no paid maternity leave may have little choice but to return to work before establishing a robust milk supply (it can take around six weeks for a mother's body to adjust to a newborn's demands). When she returns to work, she may find that federal laws protecting women's rights to breaks and a space for pumping are not respected. Not all women can afford to advocate for themselves. A new mother who fears retaliation from a noncompliant employer, unable to afford litigation and time finding new employment, might face the choice be-

tween breastfeeding her infant and continuing to feed herself and the rest of her family. A new mother who lacks
partner support for her choice to breastfeed might have
difficulty navigating early challenges with latching, over-
supply, or inverted nipples. Bottle feeding might represent blessed relief from the sheer physical pain of nursing
through cracked and bleeding nipples in a bleary-eyed,
sleep-deprived haze from hours spent up at night cradling
a colicky newborn, with cluster feedings every twenty
minutes. Given all the challenges that can arise even when
no medical condition precludes breastfeeding, mothers
need serious reasons to choose breastfeeding and substantial support to persevere through these challenges.

Mothering today may come with many more accessories than mothering of the past, but it is also a much more
isolating experience. Unlike in communal tribal villages or
even the suburbia of the 1950s, women who mother now
are likely to do so in isolation with little help from family
members, community, or even seasoned mothers to whom
they can look for guidance. Delays in childbearing age
and the move toward dual-income households mean that
the community of a new mother likely contains a greater
proportion of single women and working mothers whose
careers lessen their availability for support and companionship. A baby's grandparents, too, may still be working
and have limited availability to impart wisdom or help
with childcare — if they even live close enough to help at
all! Mothers today find themselves with more gadgets and
less personal support than ever. Additionally, women are

less well prepared for the experience of motherhood than ever before: Because we have shifted away from communal models of childcare and family sizes have declined, fewer women have spent time caring for children in their teenage and young adult years. For a significant number of new mothers, the first newborn baby they hold is their own.

And so the impetus behind the "Fed Is Best" movement is a good one. Mothers who struggle to breastfeed their children need our empathy, not judgment. That empathy is not enough, though. "Fed Is Best" offers comfort to those who are struggling to breastfeed, but the issue is too important to stop at comfort; justice demands that we seek out the source of these struggles and work toward solutions. One of the leading factors in a woman's continued breastfeeding is partner support; how do we increase that? Additional obstacles are lack of paid maternity leave and insufficient support for the physical demands of pumping in the workplace. What can we do to reshape these landscapes to make them more hospitable for mothers to do as they wish: to nourish their children in the best way possible? The way to support mothers is not by denying what we know to be true. We owe them and their children more than that.

We need to continue to better understand the benefits of breast milk and make them known to mothers, their families, employers, and policymakers. For some women, knowledge of these benefits alone will strengthen determination, providing enough motivation to overcome obstacles. And as we look to further the common good in our society, we ought to seek ways to address the obstacles that impede mothers from carrying out their breastfeeding plans or from even imagining themselves breastfeeding their infants in the first place.

The Benefits of Breastfeeding

As it turns out, breastfeeding trumps formula feeding by just about every measure, and the disparities are significant. Compared to formula-fed infants, breastfed infants enjoy a myriad of health benefits, including reduced lower respiratory tract infections, middle ear infections, allergies, and asthma.[6] Infants who are breastfed "borrow" their early immune systems from their mothers. And the benefits of breastfeeding extend beyond infancy. Longitudinal studies reveal that adults who were breastfed as infants enjoy far better health than their formula-fed counterparts, with an increased duration of breastfeeding being associated with greater benefits.[7] Breastfed infants enjoy improved neurodevelopmental outcomes, are less likely to suffer childhood cancers, are less likely to need orthodontia as teenagers, and have a reduced risk of developing obesity and diabetes as adults.[8] The longitudinal studies provide heaps of evidence that breastfeeding's long-term benefits correlate with the amount of time spent nursing: The longer women nurse their infants, the greater the benefits — including the prevention of obesity and diabetes.

It is not only infants who enjoy significant benefits from breastfeeding. Mothers who breastfeed have reduced symptoms of postpartum depression, are "more sensitive to child's needs," and have a reduced risk of developing rheumatoid arthritis, hypertension, hyperlipidemia, cardiovascular disease, heart attack, diabetes, and breast and ovarian cancer.[9] This reduction is also positively correlated with the cumulative lifetime duration of breastfeeding; in other words, the longer a woman breastfeeds (and the earlier in her life, in some cases), the lower her risks for developing these conditions in the long run. Although protection from cancer is not likely to be high on anyone's lists of top reasons for bearing a child, it might be a consideration in the timing of family planning. A woman who might otherwise postpone beginning a family until later in life may reconsider given these statistics, especially if she has a family history of one of these cancers. Women need to have access to all the facts to make truly informed decisions about childbearing.

In addition to its avalanche of health benefits, breastfeeding is beneficial to the family pocketbook as well. The US Surgeon General estimates that breastfeeding families save between $1,200 and $1,500 annually.[10] The cost of formula far outdistances that of breastfeeding, even accounting for all the optional nursing accessories on the market. Nursing covers, bottles, storage bags, and breast pumps are all *optional* for breastfeeding families (pumps, incidentally, are cost-free for families, covered at 100 percent under the Affordable Care Act).

Even adoptive and foster families can avail themselves of nutritional benefits of breast milk, although this is not always financially feasible. Banked milk costs significantly more than formula — about ten times as much, a price discrepancy akin to organic grass-fed beef versus the least expensive supermarket cuts. While some families will be able to afford this, it is a choice that is not currently a reality for all adoptive families. Nursing mothers who might like to make this more feasible for other families can connect with milk banks through sites like mothersmilk.org. The screening and donation process is free for donors, and the more supply these banks have, the more accessible this option will be for families in the future. This act of "feeding the hungry" is a corporal work of mercy that breast-feeding mothers are uniquely qualified to carry out!

Dependence on Formula Yields Corporate Profits

Not only is formula more expensive, but once families begin using it, it can be difficult to stop. Switching back and forth freely is difficult because breast milk supply relies on biofeedback to continue. Each nursing session sends signals to the mother's body about the demand for milk. Longer and more frequent feedings increase supply (this is one reason for those dreaded cluster feeding sessions when mothers may feel they are nursing almost continuously for hours on end!). Conversely, a mother's body responds to fewer feedings or feedings that are shorter in duration by decreasing supply. More feedings, more milk. Fewer feedings, less milk. Particularly for women struggling to produce milk in the first place, every feeding is crucial. Supplementing with formula begins the process of weaning, signaling to the mother's body a reduced need for milk. Women can combat this by consuming certain foods, teas, and herbs thought to increase milk production (galactagogues), and in some cases may be able to revive milk production through intentionally frequent feeding, skin-to-skin contact, and bed rest with their infants. But unless families pay careful attention to these details when supplementing with formula, supply will decrease, creating a dependence on formula.

Formula corporations in the United States attempt to create much the same dependence through direct-to-consumer marketing. The influence of the formula industry is widespread, and women receive mixed messages from governmental assistance programs and even their family doctors (not to mention well-meaning grandmothers who are statistically likely to have fed their own children with formula). The formula industry markets heavily by offering free samples through baby registry incentives, obstetricians, hospitals, and pediatrics offices. Because of the biofeedback mechanisms described above, even a little bit of formula (*especially* in the early days) can be detrimental to breast milk supply. Families determined to breastfeed through the optimal duration do not benefit by availing themselves of these "free" samples. Rather, they should recognize them as potential obstacles to their success and avoid them, making their intentions clear to all caregivers who might unintentionally sabotage their efforts through something as seemingly innocuous as giving the infant an extra feeding with formula.

While formula can be a gift to those for whom it is medically necessary, it is more often the case that this industry perpetuates itself by predatory schemes at the expense of its unwitting consumers. As a baby's need for milk will not decrease significantly until well after weaning, the use of formula creates a dependence upon it that will last through the first year. Families who are struggling financially, and even those who merely wish to avoid incurring an unnecessary expense, need this information to make informed decisions about how they feed their infants.

The only category in which formula wins is in creating value for shareholders; the industry generates $2.3 billion each year.[11] Unfortunately, this industry is yet another example of corporations marketing products that may do more harm than good to the average consumer. Let's do the math. Even if we take the 5 percent figure to be a valid measure of mothers medically unable to breastfeed, that still leaves a gap of 73 percent between those babies and the 22.3 percent of babies who are exclusively breastfed through six months.[12] Many American families are missing out on the free, natural benefits of breastfeeding while padding the pockets of the formula corporations. Those who are socioeconomically vulnerable are most at risk; infants enrolled in WIC account for 54 percent of formula consumption in the United States annually.[13] Although lack of paid maternity leave and workplace obstacles to pumping are pervasive, it is those employed in the industries that pay the least (such as the food service industry) who suffer most. Such a glaring structural injustice warrants our attention and efforts to remedy it. Mothers need to be empowered to advocate for themselves and insist that their employers adjust their policies to adhere to governmental regulations already in place, such as the break time and separate space to be provided for pumping as federally mandated by section 7 of the Fair Labor Standards Act. [14]

The Spirituality of Nursing

Even if there were no measurable, quantifiable benefits to breastfeeding, the fact remains that the nursing relationship between a mother and child is utterly beautiful. Between the tangible sign of a mother's gift of her own body to her child and the deep bonding that occurs at hormonal levels, it is no wonder that ancient Jews and early Christians alike drew on the intimacy of this relationship for rich spiritual metaphors. The Hebrew Scriptures repeatedly connect the relationship of breastfeeding and the sustaining love of God. Psalm 131:2 says, "But I have calmed and quieted my soul, / like a weaned child with its mother; / my soul is like the weaned child that is with me." Most poignantly, Isaiah 49:15 asks, "Can a woman forget her nursing child, / or show no compassion for the child of her womb?"

The early Church Fathers recognized the spiritual significance of nursing as an imitation of the sacrifice of Christ. St. John Chrysostom concluded one Good Friday homily: "As a woman nourishes her child with her own blood and milk, so does Christ unceasingly nourish with his own blood those to whom he himself has given life."[15]

Medieval Christians, especially women, were drawn to the connection between nursing and Christ's body offered in the Eucharist. They used graphic images, in art and in visions, depicting Christ as a nursing mother, in some cases with blood flowing instead of breast milk.[16] St. Catherine of Siena described visions of drinking blood from the breast of Jesus, and there are even stories of holy medieval virgins breastfeeding the faithful, in imitation of the self-offering of nourishment in Christ's body.[17] English mystic Julian of Norwich depicted Christ as mother in her *Revelations of Divine Love*, using images of conception, labor, and nursing as metaphorical expressions of His love for us.[18]

The tradition begun by ancient and medieval Christians of connecting Christ's sacrifice and the Eucharist to the physical tolls of the gift of self in motherhood continues today. Contemporary Catholic mothers echo, "This is my body, given for you," as they nurse their newborns. Popular worship artist Danielle Rose expresses the Eucharistic mystery of motherhood in these lyrics to her song, "A Mother's Communion":

> Love will lead to liberation; there's no greater love
>   than this:
> To lay down my life, to pay the real price for you,
>   little friend.
> Laboring in expectation, suffering to serve a feast
> My breast is bread, my milk is wine, for you to
>   freely come receive. ...

This is a mother's communion.
She's a chalice for her child.[19]

Reflecting on her experience of early motherhood, author Laura Kelly Fanucci recounts the physical tolls of pregnancy, labor, postpartum exhaustion, and nursing, echoing the same refrain after each: "This is my body, given for you."[20] Ginny Kubitz Moyer echoes the sentiment of Sue Monk Kidd that breastfeeding offers an "insider view" of the Eucharist: "There is something profoundly Christlike about feeding another person with your body."[21] This image resonates in the spiritual reflection of Catholic mothers who share their experiences through blogs and books. The connection between the nourishment offered at the breast and Christ's offering of His own body for us to consume resonates throughout history and continues to be a way in which women uniquely embody Christ today.

Advocating for Our Children

As well-intentioned as the "Fed Is Best" movement is, it misses the mark. In focusing our attention on mothers' feelings, it shifts our attention away from working to ensure what really is *best* for our children. Instead of rallying us to remedy injustices or break the cycles that perpetuate them, it aims for a lesser good. When we see discrepancies in the food available for children of varying socioeconomic statuses, do we remark, "Their mothers are doing their best. No need to improve the children's diet if that's all that they can afford. He is getting plenty of calories eating Frito-Lay chips and Oreos™ from the gas station. After all, fed is best"? We do not. We recognize the injustice in the disparity of available nutrition and seek to correct the deficit.

In the same way that our older children deserve access to the nutrients in fresh fruits and vegetables, our infants deserve access to the nutrients and benefits of breast milk. In this case, the issues span across race and class (although the marginalized get the short end of the stick here as well). Nonetheless, whenever a woman struggles to feed her child and cannot provide the best available form of nutrition (particularly when that form is free), it is an issue of justice. There is no shame in a mother struggling to breastfeed. There is no shame for mothers in poverty struggling to put food on the table. Both are communal failures — ones that require a response at a societal level. A movement like "Fed Is Best" is a compassionate response, but it is also too simple. It is easy to focus on rhetoric and soothing mothers' feelings of inadequacy. More difficult is the work of uncovering the real solutions this set of problems demands.

The WHO recommends that children be breastfed through the age of two. Women and their children would be better served by asking what it is about our culture that makes this feat, which has been the norm across so many generations and indigenous cultures, so much less accessible to us. The solution is not to turn a blind eye to science or ignore the medical realities, but instead to turn a hard eye on those social and cultural barriers that impede mothers from doing what is best for their children.

We need to stop pretending that man's invention can ever approximate what woman produces through her nature, and we must harness our feminine genius to envision a culture more hospitable to mothers and to the youngest members of our society. We can and should advocate on behalf of our infants.

CHAPTER 8

The Working
Mom Dilemma

A s I write this chapter, the number one new release in the Christian marriage category on Amazon is a book asserting that mothers must not work outside the home. Authored by a Catholic mother and published by a Catholic publisher, this tome represents yet another installment of this ongoing debate in Christian circles. And while this particular text is haughty and poorly researched, its initial popularity serves to show that Christian women are desperate for voices that speak to their feminine hearts amidst secular feminism's monotone drone. We know that the line that women can do it all and have it all is just that: a line. As the generation of women raised primarily by working mothers comes of age, the number of working mothers is shrinking.[1] Women whose mothers worked are less often choosing that for themselves.

While the Catholic Church has not officially weighed in on the debate over whether mothers should work outside the home, we have the witness of working-mother saints, such as pediatrician St. Gianna Molla and lace-maker St. Zélie Martin, whose lives show us that a mother's holiness is not incompatible with income-earning work. And we need the feminine genius in the workplace — especially the gift of mothers who can continue to shape a culture increasingly hospitable to families. Families must prayerfully discern how to generate income and care for their children using the resources available to them. At the same time, that discernment must take place in light of God's truth. What do the wisdom of the Church and scientific research tell us about what is really best for children? How can families use this information to discern how to best meet the needs of each member of their community of love?

A Wife of Noble Character

How does Scripture describe the ideal wife? It is worth reviewing Proverbs 31:10–31:

> A capable wife who can find?
>> She is far more precious than jewels.
>> The heart of her husband trusts in her
>> and he will have no lack of gain.

She does him good, and not harm,
all the days of her life.
She seeks wool and flax
and works with willing hands.
She is like the ships of the merchant,
she brings her food from far away.
She rises while it is still night
and provides food for her household
and tasks for her servant-girls.
She considers a field and buys it;
with fruit of her hands she plants a vineyard.
She girds herself with strength,
and makes her arms strong.
She perceives that her trading is profitable.
Her lamp does not go out at night.
She puts her hand to the distaff,
and her hands hold the spindle.
She opens her hand to the poor
and reaches out her hands to the needy.
She is not afraid for her household when it snows,
for all her household are clothed in crimson.
She makes herself coverings;
her clothing in fine linen and purple.
Her husband is known in the city gates,
taking his seat among the elders of the land.
She makes linen garments and sells them;
she supplies the merchants with sashes.
Strength and dignity are her clothing,
and she laughs at the time to come.

> She opens her mouth with wisdom,
>> and teaching of kindness is on her tongue.
> She looks well to the ways of her household,
>> and does not eat the bread of idleness.
> Her children rise up and call her happy;
>> her husband too, and he praises her:
> "Many women have done excellently,
>> but you surpass them all."
> Charm is deceitful, and beauty is vain;
>> but a woman who fears the LORD is to be
>> praised.
> Give her a share in the fruit of her hands,
>> and let her works bring her praise at the city
>> gates.

The woman in this passage fills many roles. She certainly does not "eat the bread of idleness"! Even in a culture in which women did not work for a salary outside the home, the "ideal wife" (as many translations' subheadings call her) not only cooks, cleans, and cares for her children and household but also weaves and sells linen garments; the author compares her to a merchant ship. She is active in real estate and ranching, buying and cultivating land. While the exact list of tasks may vary, contemporary mothers find that their to-do lists are similarly lengthy, including childcare, menu planning, grocery shopping, meal prepping, housekeeping, chauffeuring, educating, and so on. Despite the ways in which our culture tends to demean and devalue the work of homemaking, these tasks have dignity that ripples far beyond their temporal significance. The souls of the children we are raising will live into eternity. The question is *not* whether mothers should work; *all* mothers are *working* mothers. The debate is whether the needs of children are so great and the work of caring for them so valuable that a mother's divided attention in itself constitutes a violation of her vocational responsibilities to them.

Women in the Workplace

Despite claims to the contrary, the Church does not espouse the position that wives and mothers are relegated to certain types of work based on their gender. Rather, the most recent magisterial statements enthusiastically support women's active participation in the workforce. As noted in chapter 2, Pope Francis recently stated that "the feminine genius is needed wherever we make important decisions."[2] Pope St. John Paul II thanked mothers and working women alike in his 1995 *Letter to Women*: "You are present and active in every area of life — social, economic, cultural, artistic and political. In this way you make an indispensable contribution to the growth of a culture which unites reason and feeling, to a model of life ever open to the sense of 'mystery', to the establishment of economic and political structures ever more worthy of humanity."[3] As we saw in chapter 2, the feminine gifts of receptivity and attentiveness to persons render all human structures, from the family to corporations to governments, more nurturing and hospitable. The presence of mothers within the workplace often serves to remake those organizations in ways more deeply attuned to the needs of families.

The debate over whether mothers should work in or out of the home misses the point in several respects. First, as so many Americans learned during the stay-at-home orders of the pandemic in 2020, working at home by no means guarantees balance between childcare and job responsibilities. Children, especially young children, require our attentiveness and presence. So does quality work. It is the division of our attention — our ability to attend to the needs of children and employment simultaneously — rather than location that ought to be the determining factor in our discernment. Additionally, most mothers pursue creative projects and recreation outside of care for their children. The questions of where a woman practices these pursuits and whether they bring in income are less important than whether her children's needs — physical, spiritual, and emotional — are met.

Furthermore, mothers are not the only ones in the equation. It is the vocation of husband and wife together as partners to provide for their families. While in many cultures and throughout much of history men have primarily provided protection and income while women have taken on the lion's share of childcare, we should be careful not to impose those norms as rigid roles. When discerning how best to structure a family and raise children, the fundamental questions couples must ask are these: *Given our particular circumstances, what is in the best interest of our children? What are the resources we as a couple have to provide that?* Is it best for children to have one stay-at-home parent if it means that the other must be away on business trips, deployed, or on call? Is it better to maximize the time children have with both parents, even if it means that both parents work outside the home? These questions are best left to the prudential judgment of the parents, who can prayerfully offer the matter to the Holy Spirit and be creative in using their resources well. The ages and temperaments of the children, fiscal and psychological factors, availability of familial and social support, and demands of the job are just some of the variables couples must account for in their discernment. There is no one-size-fits-all answer because each man, woman, and child is unique and has his or her own call from God.

Vocation and Identity[4]

Motherhood is one aspect of the more expansive vocational call to marriage. One of the major flaws of the working mom dilemma is that it presupposes that any woman's identity can be reduced to her being "just a mom." To fulfill the primary aspect of their vocation, mothers must relate to their husbands first as wives and partners. The role of mother often flows from the vocation of marriage, but it is certainly not an essential aspect of the sacrament; many couples live out the call to generativity in ways other than parenthood.

More fundamentally, every woman has an identity that exists prior to and independently of her familial relationships. This identity is not subservient to motherhood. Rather, the relationship between motherhood and a woman's identity is reciprocal. Being a complete self is what allows a mother to offer self-gift in motherhood, and her motherhood in turn shapes her identity. Mothers who feel called to meaning, service, and creation beyond their children need not suffer guilt; these desires are part of who God has made them to be. This call is within the heart of every woman, regardless of her status as mother or employee, and God has designed her with the unique gifts to fulfill her unique call.

The vocation of a woman *ought to* expand beyond motherhood, because motherhood expresses only part of the God-given call of a woman. The call to develop our feminine gifts through sincere gift of self resounds in the heart of every woman. It is a call to spiritual motherhood, sometimes lived out as a natural mother and, in other cases, lived out in different relationships and types of communities (religious life, for example). Mary practiced spiritual motherhood while she was still pregnant when she drew near to Elizabeth's side at the Visitation.

Mothering children is one of the many opportunities God offers us on the path to holiness, allowing us to make use of our feminine gifts of receptivity, attentiveness, and nurturing. There are seasons, like the newborn season of early motherhood, when it can *feel* like one is "just a mom." As the intensity of needs lessens, the landscape of motherhood changes;[5] focus shifts, and other aspects of self slide back into view, like the shifting shapes in a kaleidoscope as it turns. We may not see all aspects of our identity all the time, but they are always present.

Understanding that motherhood is an *aspect* of a woman's vocation rather than its totality sheds light on the working mom dilemma. This perspective allows us to see that a mother's employment is a practical matter of *how* she is to live out her identity and vocation.

Understanding the Science

"Familial discernment" ought not to be read as code for bowing to the whims and desires of either or both parents. Discernment implies a prayerful, conscientious process; parents have the obligation to discover what is objectively best for their children and, if necessary, to make sacrifices to provide that for them. Discernment does not and cannot mean "anything goes." It must correspond to what is true and good. Research by licensed clinical social worker Erica Komisar clearly indicates that a mother's presence as primary caregiver, particularly in the first three years, is vital to a child's well-being.

Presenting a mountain of research indicating that a mother's presence, both physical and emotional, is essential, Komisar debunks the myths that quality time is more important than quantity and that any loving caregiver will do. She presents neurological research suggesting that a mother's nurturing directly affects the physical structures of the brain in critical ways, impacting emotional regulation, resilience to stress, and the ability to form deep emotional connections.[6] Her research further reveals that it does indeed matter that this nurturing comes from a *mother*, with several studies pointing to the "love hormone" oxytocin as the biological foundation for the touching, gazing, reflecting, and comforting so much more prevalent in mothers than in fathers.[7] (Masculine nurturing behaviors seen in fathers, governed by a higher presence of the hormones vasopressin and testosterone, are less empathetic but equally important. For example, rather than kissing a boo-boo, a father encourages his child to get right back up and keep exploring. A father's influence is equally important in developing a confident, independent child, as we have seen in chapter 2.)

Komisar goes on to review study after study on the influence of a mother's presence (or lack thereof) on her children's early development, positing that the dramatic increase in mental health conditions such as anxiety, depression, ADHD, and autism in children is linked to "increased maternal stress and the lack of consistent, intimate engagement of mothers."[8] For example, researchers for the American Academy of Pediatrics found that a mother's nurturing had a direct and lasting effect on her child's brain: A calm, responsive mother helped develop resilience, while neglect and insecure attachment produced a lasting, chronic stress response.[9]

These many studies point to the pervasive neurological need for the release of oxytocin in a developing brain, the strongest and most consistent source of which is a nurturing mother. The fact is that even the most attentive of paid caregivers cannot hope to approximate the bond — spiritual and *physical*, as the research shows — between mother and child. And as Komisar argues, that bond has demonstrable lifelong socio-emotional effects on our children. While others may be able to act as reasonable substitutes for limited periods of time, a mother's love and presence are irreplaceable.

Choosing the Better Part

The research is overwhelming: Children ache for attentive parents, and their well-being suffers when they are deprived of it. Quality, it seems, demands quantity as a prerequisite. In a culture that has come to rely on dual incomes, families might find themselves feeling deeply challenged by these realities. At times, we all allow lesser things to eclipse the responsibility to serve our spouses and children with the attentiveness that is appropriate to our vocational call. A mother need not be employed to cross this boundary — a boundary analogous to placing something idolatrously before God. All of us struggle to balance and prioritize our lives rightly. St. Ignatius of Loyola recognized that more often than being tempted to obvious evils, souls seeking God are "tempted under the appearance of good."[10] Even good actions attended to with holy desires can become idols if they come before God or hurt our relationships.

This was my experience as a young mother. In the early years of our marriage, my husband and I both worked. Thanks to the careful financial planning of my husband, Garrett, we had been able to afford the rent on a tiny but comfortable apartment in Southern California, pay down our substantial student loan debt, and even put a little bit away into savings each month. When our oldest daughter was born, I didn't earn much as a high school theology teacher, but it was enough that, like most American couples, we depended upon our dual-income system to maintain our lifestyle. Although we had always discussed raising our hypothetical children with a hypothetical stay-at-home mom, whenever I brought this up to my husband, his reply was the same: "We can't afford it."

During my pregnancy, I would lie awake and pray that our financial situation would change. Right up to our daughter's birth and through the next two years, I prayed novena after novena for the intention of staying home with our daughter. My heart ached when I had to leave her in the arms of another woman, and I became blindly efficient in my teaching responsibilities to free up more time to be with her. During breaks at work, I researched alternative employment opportunities and educational grants that would allow me more time with her. Throughout all of this, I suppressed a nagging truth gnawing deep in my heart: We *could* afford for me to stay home with our daughter. It just wasn't enough of a priority for us.

This truth I refused to acknowledge was part of the reason my heart ached so much when I relinquished my daughter to the care of another mother each day. She was free to take care of my daughter during the workday because *she* stayed home with her children. Her family crammed into an apartment half the size of ours in a significantly sketchier complex. She walked to the grocery store because they had only one car. Her family was clearly making financial sacrifices that we refused to make.

When I brought up our comparative situations to my husband, he would point out that neither of them had gone to college, and so had no massive student loan debts hanging over their heads. Their choices were also unwise, he argued. My husband's childhood had been ravaged by financial insecurity. The anxiety of living with an addict who rarely worked and drained the family finances never truly left him, even when his father did. He grew up watching his mother struggle to make ends meet working part-time shifts at Albertsons and, on more than one occasion, gambling to try to make the mortgage payments. Although he never truly had to do without, he grew up in an environment of pervasive instability.

Many families face adversity in a way that draws them together, strengthening their reliance on one another and their trust in God. That was not Garrett's experience. As a child who wasn't privy to the real reason behind his family's financial struggles, he absorbed the idea that financial insecurity was what caused his world to crumble. He vowed that his family would never suffer in the same way. His marriage would be successful because he would provide. His children would feel secure and cherished because he would never allow his family's security to unravel in the same way. Consequently, financial security has become simultaneously one of the greatest gifts he provides us and one of his biggest roadblocks to trusting in God.

So this was our struggle. Despite having a significantly larger income than this other family, we couldn't "afford" for me to stay home because it left us with too small a margin to pay our bills. What if Garrett lost his job? What if we could never save enough to buy a house? What if? What if.

An image that is often used to describe our worldly attachments, our inability to relinquish sin, is that of a monkey trap, a narrow-necked jar in which the hunter places a piece of fruit like an orange. The orange fits in easily on its own, but when the monkey reaches in to grasp it, the added width of his hand makes it difficult to withdraw the fruit. He is stuck. If he simply relinquished his grasp on the prize, he would be free. But he will not, and so the monkey is caught.

Our failure to relinquish our grasp on security is not all on Garrett's shoulders. My own limitations played their part. Had I not been so consumed with my desire for his approval, had I been more vocal about my deep desire to be home with our daughter, had I been willing to risk some conflict in our marriage for the sake of open communication, things might have gone very differently.

And they did two years later, when our second child was born. I communicated clearly desires I assumed my husband had been aware of since I became a mother. Once he understood that I viewed being at home with our children as an essential aspect of my motherhood, a desire deeper than my career or educational pursuits, he set to work. He refinanced our house and rearranged our assets.

He got creative and cut our expenses to degrees that my coupon cutting never could have. After I quit my job, we had seven dollars left over from each paycheck. The temptation is to view this as a tight margin, but that is a matter of perspective. After all, we not only had *enough*; we had money *left over*.

Openness to the Spirit

Some have a tendency to relativize this discussion, to speak as though all choices are equal and the self-actualization of the mother or her feelings of fulfillment are the bottom line. *This is a lie.* So is the claim that mothers are called to forgo service to the world outside their homes and families. Neither extreme is sufficient to express what God has created in women. The wisdom that comes with motherhood, and the feminine genius[11] more broadly, are essential in every realm of public life.

Even in hindsight, it is difficult to evaluate the choices our family made. Did continuing to work objectively contribute to the highest likelihood of benefit to our daughter? Clearly not, given the research laid out in this chapter. Still, that consideration was only one piece — albeit a significant one — of the much larger puzzle of our lives. As a mom, I wanted to be home. But as my husband's wife, I deferred to my husband's judgment despite my heartache. Had I insisted on quitting my job against his wishes, it would have fractured our relationship. It was the right choice for our marriage, and so for our family.

God's plans are so much larger than the narrow vision

we have for ourselves; we need to create space for prayer and discernment to be open to the ways His Spirit is moving in each family's particular circumstances. In our case, He brought immense and beautiful blessings out of that time. Our need for childcare drove us to invite our extended family into our lives in a more intimate way than we otherwise might have; when Garrett's grandmother graciously watched our daughter one day a week, I grew to love her more deeply and even ended up sponsoring her when she entered the Church a few years later. I met my dearest friend, my soul friend, during that time. She has been a listening ear, comrade in the trenches, a role model, and inspiration in faith and in motherhood. It was during that time that I earned my degrees in theology and bioethics, pursuits that would have been financially out of reach without the aid I received as a teacher. In many ways, this book itself and the opportunity to share our family's story is a fruit of that time and education.

We don't always recognize all the ways God is moving in our lives, and when we do, that insight often comes much later, when the dust has settled and the storms have passed. When it comes to deciding familial structures, habits, and rhythms, there is much more room for discernment than we often realize. Of course, God's Word and the plans He has revealed for our lives should be at the center (see chapter 3). Beyond that, we should be careful not to absolutize our *own* discernment by imposing it upon others. It may not always be possible for single parents and families of limited means to arrange their lives to maximize presence to their children and earn a living wage. The same degree of choice is not available to us all. We need to spend less time making prescriptions for other families[12] and more time reveling in the joy of caring for our own. When that joy bubbles over to other work (paid or not), and when that other work allows us to return to our families more ourselves, with more to give, we know that we have found a beautiful balance.

Responding Faithfully to the Cross of Infertility (and Why It Doesn't Include IVF)

Much of God's truth about who we are is written into our bodies. With fertility built into our bodies, is it any wonder that God placed it deep within our hearts as well? Scripture expounds the blessing that children are to faith-filled couples: "Your children will be like olive shoots around your table" (Ps 128:3). Before being admitted to the Sacrament of Matrimony, couples must attest that they will willingly accept children as gifts from God. So much of our Catholic faith and culture surrounding the vocation of marriage preoccupies itself with children and parenthood. And yet many couples struggle to conceive and bear children. Considering their own heartfelt desires and the deeply ingrained social and religious expectations that they become parents, how are Catholic couples to faithfully respond to infertility?

This chapter and chapter 10 are dedicated in response to this question. In this chapter, we will address questions about infertility within marriage and the Church's position on *in vitro* fertilization [IVF] based on the marriage covenant and the dignity of those involved. Chapter 10 will deal with the ethical issues that arise when would-be parents, however well-intentioned, commandeer the biological materials and faculties of others — namely the donation of gametes (eggs and sperm) and gestational surrogacy (the renting of a woman's womb) — for the creation of children.

One of the most painful crosses families are asked to bear is the struggle of infertility. The burdens of this struggle weigh heavily on both men and women, for whom infertility seems to strike at the heart of their identity in different ways. Men feel impotent and emasculated, unable to provide their wives with the desires of their hearts. Women grapple with feelings of betrayal by their own bodies as they fail to do what they are made to do. A woman's capacity to bring forth life is one of her most basic defining capabilities, one that she nurtures each month for most of her adult life — enduring hormonal surges, pains, and bleeding over which she has no control in preparation to receive the gift of life, her child, inside her womb. That womb's continued emptiness with the return of each cycle serves as a continual reminder of the growing space in her heart and her arms waiting to embrace a child. For couples wrestling with seemingly endless cycles of hope and disappointment, IVF can seem like a light at the end of the tunnel, a way to leverage technological advances to gain control of an uncertain and at times heart-wrenching process.

It is difficult to understand how God is at work for good here, though we know from His words in Scripture and the witness of the saints that He is. More difficult, perhaps, is to trust in the goodness of the moral guidelines of the Church, whose dictates rule out paths that might otherwise aid couples struggling to conceive. While many are aware of the Church's stance on IVF, some assume it to be the outdated position of an ancient organization unable to keep pace with the times. However, the reality is that the Church prohibits the use of IVF not in reaction to its novelty, but out of convictions that have existed for hundreds of years, convictions that continue to hold weight even in the face of new technological capabilities.

A Breach of Marital Unity and Fidelity

The Church's arguments against IVF stem from her teachings about the meaning and purpose of sexual intimacy. The marital embrace serves a purpose that is twofold, existing both for the sake of marital unity and for procreation. The *Catechism of the Catholic Church* explains that "in marriage, the physical intimacy of the spouses becomes a sign and pledge of spiritual communion."[1] To separate these two purposes of sexual union is to divide the sign of the sacrament and is therefore a violation of the marital covenant.

Pope St. John Paul II explains the integration of the spiritual and physical union of the marital act this way in his apostolic exhortation on the family:

> Sexuality, by means of which man and woman give themselves to one another through the acts which are proper and exclusive to spouses, is by no means something purely biological, but concerns the innermost being of the human person as such. … The total physical self-giving would be a lie if it were not the sign and fruit of a total personal self-giving, in which the whole person, including the temporal dimension, is present: if the person were to withhold something or reserve the possibility of deciding otherwise in the future, by this very fact he or she would not be giving totally.
>
> This totality which is required by conjugal love also corresponds to the demands of responsible fertility. This fertility is directed to the generation of a human being, and so by its nature it surpasses the purely biological order and involves a whole series of personal values. For the harmonious growth of these values a persevering and unified contribu-

tion by both parents is necessary.[2]

The total gift of self in marriage climaxes in the union of the sexual embrace, a reality that is at once physical, biological, and spiritual. Prior to the invention of IVF, the only way in which to separate the pleasurable, unifying aspect of sex from its procreative power was through contraception. For the bulk of human history, there was no way to procreate apart from the physically unitive marital act (even though the act itself did not always take place between spouses, constituting its own violation of the sanctity of marriage). The development of reproductive technologies has brought with it the possibility of this separation. Though the technology is new, the argument stands: Severing the dual purposes of the marital act diminishes the dignity of the act and that of the marriage covenant.

For couples who desperately desire to grow their families, this argument can seem esoteric and disconnected from lived experience. Surely whatever minor harms come from using this new technology cannot possibly outweigh the heart-wrenching pain of infertility? This line of thought is particularly tempting when the reproductive act has shifted from its traditional context within the sexual act into the hands of technicians. This clinicalization of reproduction disguises the fact that the couple has invited a third party (and sometimes many more parties) into the intimacy of their marriage. While most couples acknowledge that it is a violation of their vows to invite third parties into their bedroom to attempt conception the natural way, the problem with doing so in a laboratory is more obscure.

While it is clear that sexual intimacy with another violates our vows of fidelity, it is less clear to us how assisted reproduction does so when the sexual embrace is not involved (even less so when that third party helps the couple to reproduce *with one another*). After all, doctors assist us with all kinds of bodily functions. In an age of easy access to medical care, it seems only natural to seek a doctor's assistance in restoring our bodily functions. This line of thinking seems quite reasonable, and indeed it would be if reproduction were a mere matter of bodily function. To the degree that that is the case, it is entirely permissible to seek intervention. Generally speaking, medical treatments that work to heal the body or restore it to full functioning belong to the realm of medical care and do not constitute an intrusion of a third party into the marital act. There are many ways doctors may licitly intervene to promote the health of both partners to facilitate conception. They may prescribe hormones or fertility medication, surgically correct structural problems, or work to heal fertility-limiting conditions like endometriosis or polycystic ovarian syndrome (PCOS). However, "treatments" that blur the line between medical technician and something more, a sort of "co-conceiver," violate the bonds of marital intimacy established by our Creator. Further thought and reflection are required to understand why reproduction, and not merely sexual intercourse, belongs solely between the spouses.

Conception of a new human life and the creation of a family are not mere medical processes, but spiritual dimensions of the human experience that ought not to be reduced to the bodily systems involved, as though the begetting of human life could be reduced to the breeding of animals. No, the joining of man and woman to become one flesh is the outward sign of a union much deeper than sex. This sacred, spiritual reality demands totality and exclusivity. *Donum Vitae* elaborates on this point by drawing on the language of the body. As humans are beings unified in body and soul, the meaning of the conjugal act is tied to this unity:

> Spouses mutually express their personal love in the "language of the body" which clearly involves both "spousal meanings" and parental ones. The conjugal act by which the couple mutually express their self-gift at the same time expresses openness to the gift of life. It is an act that is inseparably corporal and spiritual. It is in their bodies and through their bodies that the spouses consummate their marriage and are able to become father and mother. In order to respect the language of their bodies and their natural generosity, the conjugal union must take place with respect for its openness to procreation; and the procreation of a person must be the fruit and the result of married love. The origin of the human being thus follows from a procreation that is "linked to the union, not only biological but

also spiritual, of the parents, made one by the bond
of marriage." *Fertilization achieved outside the bodies of the couple remains by this very fact deprived of
the meanings and the values which are expressed in
the language of the body and in the union of human
persons.*[3]

For those who acknowledge the gravity of violating our
Creator's objective purpose for marriage, this may be
enough. It may be sufficient to understand that reproductive technologies detract from marital unity and lessen the
true gift of self expressed by the language of the body in
the conjugal act. The rest of us, though, might need more
convincing. In the absence of a similar moral intuition
about the wrongness of sexual infidelity, we need to spell
out the exact harms of this "reproductive infidelity." Is it
fair to call it that, as *Donum Vitae* seems to suggest here?
Because this technology is such a new development in human history, and so few of us have intimate knowledge of
its concrete effects on marriage and the family, it is more
difficult to imagine the harms that result. Certainly, it is
difficult to imagine that any of these concerns could outweigh the concrete joy of holding a long-awaited baby in
one's arms.

One way IVF detracts from unity in marriage is by
isolating one partner or the other as "the problem." Medically speaking, such isolation is necessary to diagnose the
source of the problem so that it can be treated. If the reproductive defect is found in one of the spouses, the proper

recourse is to seek healing for that spouse and restore the reproductive functioning of the couple to its full potential. This is all well and good. IVF contradicts marital unity either by the invitation of the technician into the intimacy of procreation through artificial insemination, or else by the introduction of a donor who replaces the contributions of the infertile spouse. Some argue that this is a generous allowance on the part of the infertile spouses who, by removing themselves from the equation, free their partners to achieve *their* dreams of a biologically-related child. Such so-called generosity reflects a relinquishing of the marital debt on the part of the infertile party that ought never to be accepted by a spouse, whose marital role is total acceptance of the self-gift of the other. The mere consent of a spouse cannot make procreation with a third party any more acceptable than it can render adultery innocuous.

The choice to procreate without one's spouse is the very definition of divisive. It constitutes a refusal to remain in solidarity with one's spouse in his or her struggles. Refusing to accept the limitation of one's infertile spouse is as serious as a refusal to accept the fruitfulness of a fertile partner by using contraception. Morally and relationally speaking, it is the *couple* who is infertile. Whatever the medical cause of that infertility, it is infinitely more conducive to the unity of the partners to embrace and carry the cross of infertility together than it is to leave one's partner behind and forge ahead without him or her. Actress Gabrielle Union poignantly illustrates the pain that results from such arrangements when relaying her experience of turning to surrogacy with husband Dwyane Wade. She describes herself sobbing at her surrogate's ultrasound, not tears of joy as those around her assumed, but of deep sorrow:

> This growing bump that everyone thought I wanted to see was now a visual manifestation of my failure. ... I smiled, wanting to show I — we — were so happy and grateful. But part of me felt more worthless. ... Dwyane took my hand, and there was so much happiness on his face, I lost it. My cry was a choke stopped up in my throat, tears streaming down. It was grief. I'd had so many miscarriages ... looking at the screen, I understood how many potential babies I had lost. That's why I was crying. ... The experience of Dwyane having a baby so easily — while I was unable to — left my soul not just broken into pieces but shattered into fine dust scattering in the wind.[4]

The reality is that God designed sexual intercourse for the unity of the couple. That unity is achieved by pleasurable bonding effects, hormonal and emotional, as well as by the unity of the two becoming one flesh in the reality of their biological child. Even in adoption, couples are drawn together in unity (despite the child being biologically unrelated to either spouse) because their experience in becoming parents is one in which they *share*; both spouses together accept another's child as their own, a generous act of love in which they partake in equal measure.

In Vitro Exploitation

In addition to violating the marital relationship, IVF poses further ethical problems in failing to uphold the dignity of mothers and the embryos conceived. The procedure treats women as objects for experimentation. Despite "success" rates being so low that the procedure would never receive approval as a drug for treatment of illness, IVF has managed to remain acceptable medical practice. Its rates of successful births have improved somewhat over the years (though they remain dismally low, around 30 percent) as researchers have been able to exploit the emotional vulnerabilities of women.[5] The industry dangles the hope of children, enticing women to pay their *own* way to become research subjects for the very technology they are supporting.

While the fertility industry likes to promote IVF as *the* solution to infertility, the numbers don't lie: IVF helps only 0.44 percent of the 6.7 million women struggling with infertility each year.[6] Leah Jacobson comments on IVF's shortcomings: "The reality is, IVF falls tremendously short as a solution for infertility because it does not seek to identify the root causes of infertility; instead, it attempts to bypass them. If the problem is a hormonal imbalance, endometriosis, cysts, or a number of other problems, IVF does nothing to correct those problems."[7] The expense and health risks of IVF are particularly unjust when considered in the light of alternatives like NaProTechnology.

While IVF seeks to circumnavigate the root causes of infertility, achieving conception and implantation *in spite of* existing pathologies, NaPro is a natural alternative that seeks to *heal* underlying issues that interfere with healthy pregnancies. This might be as simple as supplementation with progesterone or as complex as surgery for endometriosis, for example. Because NaPro addresses therapeutic needs of individual patients, it is not a one-size-fits-all approach. While a single cycle of IVF costs upward of $12,000 out of pocket with a success rate of 30 percent, NaPro is over 80 percent effective, with the costs of most procedures being covered under basic insurance policies.[8] The sad reality is that with big money to be made in fertility clinics and comparatively little money to be made by promoting more modest options, few doctors are even aware of the NaPro alternative.

By far the greatest cost of IVF is paid by most of the embryos conceived, who are rarely treated with human dignity or even the "special respect" (whatever that means) recommended by the US President's Council on Bioethics.[9] Many of the embryos conceived through IVF are destined to become not someone's cherished child, but merely collateral damage.

Because of the great expense of IVF, it is more efficient for clinics to create and transfer many embryos at once. While this increases the likelihood of a couple welcoming a healthy baby, the odds of any one embryo being selected, successfully transferred, and eventually born are dismal. Those conceived with genetic conditions that can be identified through the use of preimplantation genetic diagnosis are systematically discarded by technicians (although there are debates as to the right of parents to intentionally bring disabled children into the world, such as a deaf couple who wish to have a child similar themselves in that impairment).

Yet even embryos fortunate enough to be selected for implantation are not in the clear. When too many of these embryos successfully implant, a mother might find herself pregnant with three or four babies. Because multiple pregnancies are riskier for all involved and the goal is one healthy child, some numbers of successfully implanted embryos are chosen for "selective reduction." In other words, some of the embryos are aborted in the hopes that the remaining one or two will have a better chance at a healthy birth.

Embryos that survive past the preimplantation genetic diagnosis but are not selected for implantation are frozen for possible future use. So long as there is no problem with the power to the freezer (accidental thawing does sometimes occur), embryos may remain frozen indefinitely. When a couple decides they have no further desire to pursue IVF with their embryos, they may be thawed and discarded, donated for research purposes, or even "adopted" by women who use IVF to bring them to term and raise them as their own. The Church officially addressed embryo adoption in *Dignitas Personae*, concluding that using frozen embryos as a "treatment" for infertility involves ethical breaches similar to those of surrogacy. Abandoned embryos are in "a *situation of injustice which in fact cannot be resolved.*"[10]

Grieving What Is Lost, Finding a Way Forward

Couples who struggle with infertility may acknowledge truth and wisdom in the Church's guidance surrounding IVF, but they may just as likely feel betrayed and abandoned by these limitations on their options. For couples who have tried and found so many doors closed to them, leaving this stone unturned feels like giving up. Moving forward from infertility requires surrender. Acceptance of God's will is difficult any time it runs contrary to one's own desires, but especially in the case of infertility, when what we desire is good and we cannot see or understand God's purpose for allowing such a painful struggle. To acknowledge that His ways are not our ways, to accept a plan for one's life that appears very different from one's deepest hopes, requires strong and sincere faith. If God has willed us into marriage, couples ask themselves, why does He *not* will children for us?

This question lies at the center of the struggles of many faith-filled women in Scripture. We hear their fervent prayers as well as stories of their joy after so much waiting and anticipation. Sarah, Rachel, Hannah, Elizabeth, and by tradition even Mary's mother, Saint Anne, ached with desire for the children who would eventually be born to them. Companionship and solidarity with these holy women may be a deep source of consolation for women bearing similar crosses.

My husband and I have four children whom we did not struggle to conceive, though I wouldn't describe the pregnancies or births as easy. Due to genetic conditions, my prenatal care is classified as "high risk," requiring twice daily injections in my stomach. My second pregnancy involved life-threatening blood clots in my lungs, and my youngest son was born at the height of the pandemic while I labored alone, mask on, for several hours before undergoing an emergency C-section in a room full of strangers. My husband was barred from the delivery room and my infant son whisked away immediately after birth for his own "protection." Any future pregnancies will be even riskier, as the risks of my conditions (and the risks of pregnancy in general) increase with age. Birth by cesarean is especially risky with my conditions; so is vaginal birth after C-section (VBAC). But the position we find ourselves in now, yearning for more children but hesitant to expose our family to the degree of risk another pregnancy would entail, is a pale shadow of the struggle with infertility.

Before we were married, I coerced my future husband into promising me that if we could not have children, we would adopt. As an idealistic college sophomore, I viewed our future with rose-colored glasses. I lacked the maturity to grasp the monumental undertaking that is real-world adoption. I didn't see the exorbitant cost or degree of complication that arises for children who've experienced trauma. I would have refused to acknowledge that biracial adoption might come with its own set of challenges and dismissed navigating relationships with birth parents as easily managed. I knew nothing of the heartbreak of holding a long-awaited baby in your arms for a short while and then relinquishing him back into his mother's arms when she decides she wants to be his mother after all.

Though I now have a much more realistic grasp of the complexity of adoption, a process filled with unnerving unknowns and its own particular set of risks for heartbreak, these facts do not deter me. If anything, becoming a mother of four has taught me that each time we welcome a new person into our world, we welcome the unknown. Each of us is a gamble. Each child comes with his own set of peculiarities, his own joys and challenges.

It is too easy to urge couples who face infertility, having exhausted all licit medical options, special diets, and sure-thing novenas, to "simply" adopt. Adoption is not simple. What may bear fruit, though, is further reflection on our own desires to become parents. The relationship, the real work, the *substance*, of parenthood consists much more in our actions than in our genetics. The joy of shared family life is the result of daily living and loving one another and is not limited to DNA. Every adoption begins with loss — for children, who lose their place with their biological parents, as well as for adoptive parents, who let go of the future they'd pictured, dreaming about whether a child might inherit his mother's gift for song or his father's freckles. And while that loss must be grieved, it remains true for all parents that our children will turn out differently than we expected. In adoption, the experience of this reality comes much sooner. Still, adoption retrieves the dream of happy, loving family communities for both parents and children for whom it once appeared out of reach, and with nothing discernibly lacking in comparison with families created in the natural way. While families created through adoption may face a set of challenges that they do not have in common with natural families, the fact is that each family comes with its own unique crosses to bear, and it is in bearing them together that we carry out God's mission of love uniquely entrusted to us.

Spiritual Motherhood Is Not a Consolation Prize

There are couples who experience infertility and discern that adoption is not God's call for them. Although their lives may unfold in ways radically different from what they had once imagined, the call to generative love remains. One such couple was Mary Luisa Josefa and her husband, Pascual Rojas. Married in Mexico in 1881, the couple tried for many years to have children before deciding that the poor would be their children. They dedicated their marriage to serving their community, founding the Hospital of the Sacred Heart. After just fourteen years of marriage, Maria Luisa found herself a widow. She joined the Carmelites before founding her own congregation in 1921, becoming Mother Luisita, foundress of the Carmelite Sisters of the Most Sacred Heart. Although her life undoubtedly turned out much differently than she'd expected it to, Mother Luisita served God as she was uniquely created to do. Though her path to sainthood was not without sorrow, her *motherhood* has touched thousands, and her spiritual legacy lives on through the sisters still active in her community today.

The heart of every woman is the heart of a mother. This is who we have been created to be. Whatever task God calls us to complete, we complete it as spiritual mothers whose gentle presence, receptivity, and attention to the personal are indispensable in this world. Though we may not understand God's purposes, our challenge as people of faith is to entrust ourselves to Him, difficult as this may be. Whatever God works, it is for our good.

G. K. Chesterton tells us, "The way to love anything is to realize it may be lost." This sentiment resonates deeply with those who have been widowed, lost children, experienced the grief of miscarriage, or felt the pain of extended waiting for a spouse or children. When a thing is difficult to come by, we hold it all the more dear. It may be that the pain of the moment prepares us for some future task, a call for which God equips us even in our darkest hours. Perhaps it serves to open our hearts to adoption, preparing us to become stewards of the soul God has selected for us. Perhaps, as with Mother Luisita, He may direct our mother's heart toward another task entirely. It may be that this intimate experience of longing for a child prepares us to weather the tough road ahead.

In the darkness, it can be so difficult to maintain faith that the sun will rise. But rise it will, because it is the sun, and that is its nature. God is God, and His nature is goodness. Although we may not see the purpose God is working in our hearts, we know that eventually the dawn will break. Sometimes our only recourse in the midst of this kind of pain is to cry out along with Jesus in the garden: "Father … remove this cup from me; yet, not what I want, but what you want" (Mk 14:36).

The Dark Realities of Gamete Donation and Surrogacy

As with IVF within marriage, what is at stake in the ethics of gamete donation and surrogacy is a conflict between pursuing the good of fertility and more vital and fundamental goods — those of human dignity and the integrity of the marital relationship. The practices of gamete donation and surrogacy violate both of the latter for the sake of the former, and therefore cannot be accepted.

In addition to the wisdom and guidance the Church provides, this chapter explores some deeply compelling arguments for avoiding surrogacy and gamete donation that do not require an appeal to Revelation. Natural law is sufficient to demonstrate that many of these practices compromise or even gravely undermine human dignity. Given a basic belief in the inherent dignity of persons, people of every faith and none can share the Church's position based on reason alone. This makes it an exciting opportunity to link arms with feminists and others with whom the Church usually finds herself in opposition. This point of common ground provides a rare opportunity to seek justice together.

Before we begin, it is necessary to clarify two essential points. The first is that gamete donation and surrogacy are inherently exploitative and degrading practices that, like abortion, so diminish the personhood of all involved that they cannot be permitted in good conscience. However, the second point is that the following reflections serve to defend the dignity of women and children, *not* to accuse or condemn women who act as surrogates or infertile couples who cling to the hope that these women may be able to provide the child for whom they so desperately hope. To those who find themselves in these positions, we ought to offer our empathy and support, continuing to search for ways to aid them that can meet their needs and desires while upholding human dignity.

The Church on Gamete Donation and Surrogacy

The Church articulates her condemnation of gamete donation and surrogacy in *Donum Vitae*, a 1987 document that addresses contemporary questions of artificial reproduction. The term "surrogacy" applies to any pregnancy in which the mother who carries the child (conceived using her own eggs, those of the intended mother, or those of another woman altogether) has, from the outset of the pregnancy, the intention of surrendering that child to another set of parents upon birth. *Donum Vitae* recognizes the grave violations these practices involve:

> Surrogate motherhood represents an objective failure to meet the obligations of maternal love, of conjugal fidelity and of responsible motherhood; it offends the dignity and the right of the child to be conceived, carried in the womb, brought into the world and brought up by his own parents; it sets up, to the detriment of families, a division between the physical, psychological and moral elements which constitute those families. …
>
> Civil law cannot grant approval to techniques of artificial procreation which … take away what is a right inherent in the relationship between spouses; and therefore civil law cannot legalize the donation of gametes between persons who are not legitimately united in marriage. Legislation must also prohibit, by virtue of the support which is due to the family, embryo banks, *post mortem* insemination and "surrogate motherhood."[1]

In other words, surrogacy and gamete donation violate

God's plans for motherhood and the family and fail to uphold the rights and dignity of the child. How and why this is should be readily apparent, given what God has revealed regarding for marriage and the family, as discussed in chapter 3.

Defining Our Terms

The terms "egg donation" and "sperm donation" not only merit but beg for correction. "Donation" is a misnomer; when what is given is one's own future child, what occurs is not a donation, a bestowing of an object one no longer desires to possess. Rather, it is a kind of pre-adoption in which one's child is promised to another prior to the child's conception. Yet this, too, fails to capture the reality. Adoption provides a happy ending to a less-than-ideal situation and is governed by the ethics of rescue. It is something else entirely to intentionally create such a break in our familial structures. Gamete "donation" is not a fairy tale. There can be no happy ending when a child is created for the purpose of abandonment by his biological parents. In a perverse real-life version of Rumpelstiltskin, egg and sperm donors promise to surrender their future children, accepting "reasonable sums" rather than spun gold. Yet, despite its misleading characterization of the action undertaken, "donation" is the prevailing term. As "donation" is such a poor approximation of the act and, further, implies that money does not change hands, we ought to instead use market terms that more accurately represent the monetary exchange for bodily goods that the fertility industry currently relies upon to amass billions of dollars annually.

Against Obtaining and Selling Sperm

Even were it not dealing in the trade of one's future children, the procurement and selling of sperm would be incompatible with the moral teachings of the Catholic Church, many other Christian denominations, and traditional branches of the Jewish and Muslim faiths. As Catholic author Fiorella Nash observes, "The man's contribution [to IVF] invariably involves masturbating into a container with the assistance of pornographic materials that objectify and degrade women — even the male act in IVF is antiwoman."[2] Anyone of goodwill who rightly recognizes pornography for the public health crisis that it is sees the deeply problematic nature of the way sperm is collected for IVF.

And if it weren't enough to barter offspring for a paltry sum, or for a doctor to encourage the use of materials that are gravely undermining society's health and function, sperm banks then classify the product according to its market value.

Of course, that all assumes that clients receive the sperm they selected in the first place. Hundreds of plaintiffs in Canada are awaiting the results of a class action suit against Dr. Norman Barwin for using his own or unknown sperm for their inseminations.[3] Victims of doctors who, like Dr. Barwin, used their own sperm rather than the intended sample are fighting back through the website DonorDeceived.org, which documents known cases of donor fraud domestically in the US and internationally. The Netflix documentary *Our Father* details one US fertility doctor who fraudulently inseminated patients with his own sperm, resulting in at least ninety-four children, a number that continues to grow as more of his patients' children discover this shocking information via at-home DNA test kits. (Related concerns over the lack of genetic diversity when too many children are conceived from sperm from a single donor are covered in chapter 11). Unfortunately, tales of this nature are all too common, whether due to gross negligence or laboratory mix-ups. The only recourse couples have is litigation: Parents can sue their doctors for "wrongful life."

Filing a suit of this nature requires that parents state for the court that they would not have brought their child into being given full knowledge of the situation. In essence, this type of suit is one in which the primary "damage" is the existence of one's child. Whatever damage such a claim might inflict on the emotional well-being of the child, parents who sue for wrongful life at the very least secure a hefty college fund for the child, potentially compensating for the fact that his IQ wasn't precisely what they ordered

The Risks to Women of Egg Procurement

Female candidates for egg "donation" are likely to be assessed by similar criteria as men for the value of their genetic material (IQ, race, appearance, etc.), with one notable difference. Because the process of egg procurement is much more demanding and physically involved, the ideal candidate is one who can be enticed by financial compensation for the hardships endured. In other words, it is easier to convince (read: coerce) women who are at a financial disadvantage. Before we discuss the ethical ramifications of the exploitation of these women, let's first look at the process by which doctors harvest a woman's eggs for insemination.

Egg collection is an extensive medical process requiring massive doses of hormones to stimulate the ovaries to release ten to twenty eggs (significantly more than the one to two eggs the woman's ovaries release naturally each cycle), followed by a surgical procedure to procure those eggs. Despite often being touted as "low-risk" by the clinics that profit from this procurement process, the procedure can have deadly complications. The most serious risk is ovarian hyperstimulation syndrome (OHSS), which affects 5 to 10 percent of donors and most often affects women under thirty (the target age range for egg donors). Symptoms and complications include nausea, vomiting, kidney failure, blood clots, burst cysts requiring surgery, and, in less than 1 percent of women, death.[4] The long-term risks are largely unknown due to donor anonymity and lack of longitudinal studies. Considering the health risks posed by other uses of hormones — the links of hormonal contraceptives to cancer and potentially lethal blood clots[5] — it is a fair guess that the high doses of hormones involved in the procurement of eggs carry similar risks. Anecdotally, egg donors have reported long-term effects ranging from loss of fertility to breast and colon cancer. Without long-term studies, however, the safety of egg donation simply cannot be determined.[6] Despite concerns about this lack of information being raised by feminists and in major publications such as *The Washington Post*[7] and *The New York Times*[8] for years, we still lack solid answers to offer women.

Disclosure of risk varies widely across clinics. Some advertise the risks as "equal to those in IVF for intended mothers." The risks ought to be the same, as the procedures are identical. One clinic may claim the process is "very safe" with "no known long-term adverse effects" to the donor;[9] another discloses permanent changes to ovulation;[10] another lists OHSS and death as possibilities.[11] One Beverly Hills clinic entices women to become donors using intentionally misleading information, touting claims such as "Your ovarian reserve and future fertility are unaffected" and "The American Society of Reproductive Medicine has found that there is no reason to believe that it can cause long-term negative health effects."[12] That same company suggests women use their compensation from the sale to finance preemptive freezing of their own eggs for future use[13] — a clever strategy for cycling those funds back into the pockets of the fertility clinic and securing future IVF clients all at the same time.

The expense of egg freezing is more commonly being covered and promoted by Big Tech companies seeking to support the delay of childbirth. It is difficult to see how egg freezing can be justified as a health benefit, given that, in addition to the risks of the egg extraction process, delaying childbirth results in the natural *decline* in a woman's fertility and increases the likelihood of serious risk to mother and child associated with increased maternal age during pregnancy. Exactly what kind of benefit is this, and for whom?

Motherhood Dissected

Many of the issues that arise with the sale of gametes apply to surrogacy. In addition to those issues, surrogacy—whether it uses eggs from the intended mother, a donor, or the surrogate herself—violates marital unity (see "The Church on Gamete Donation and Surrogacy"). The practice of surrogacy, moreover, both robs the child of the familial stability he is owed from the outset of his existence, as argued in *Donum Vitae,* and fractures our understanding of motherhood.

The splintering of motherhood is evidenced by the number of new terms necessary to describe maternal relationships to the child. The role of mother previously filled by a single woman is divided into different tasks now fulfilled by multiple women. The intended, or social, mother takes responsibility for raising the child. The biological mother provides the raw material for the creation of the child. The gestational, or surrogate, mother is the vessel in which the embryo grows to term. Sometimes these roles remain partially united, such as when a surrogate contributes her own eggs to the embryo she grows, or when the intended mother gestates an embryo from "donated" material. Still, the fracturing is such that each of these roles *could* be fulfilled by a different woman, and our language has come to reflect these divisions of motherhood.

On top of that, the legal process has come to adjudicate varying values to these motherly roles. Social motherhood, it appears, far outweighs the claims of biological or gestational motherhood. Whether this is because of the gravity of the role itself or because of the deep litigious pockets of the consumer is arguable. The fact is that the concerns, desires, and legitimacy of the social mother — "the buyer" — nearly always trump any concerns, claims, or rights that arise in conflicts with the gestational mother — "the help." In many instances, we are seeing biological and gestational mothers literally erased from the paperwork, with only the intended mother's name appearing on the birth certificate. Not only does this lie fail to acknowledge the dignity and personhood of the women involved, but it denies the value of the women whose bodies and labor constitute their objective and incredibly tangible parental relationships with the children to be born.

We cannot deny that from the moment of conception, the surrogate alone bears responsibility for the child she nurtures within. A pregnant mother's body works unceasingly for nine months to support her growing baby. No aspect of her life is unaffected, though the physical and emotional symptoms vary from woman to woman. It is a job without breaks that ends only through the demanding climax of labor. The growing child is entirely dependent upon her, and all his interactions are mediated through her. Actions she takes have potential for benefit or harm: Her exercise improves the health of the child; her cigarette-smoking habit conveys serious risks. Her emotional well-being also affects the child she bears. High levels of anxiety experienced by pregnant mothers change the environment in which their children grow with far-reaching effects for those children, including on physical health, birth weight, mental health, behavioral effects, metabolism, and incidence of physical deformities.[14]

The Inherent Exploitation of Surrogacy

As much as we might like to believe that our conceptions of motherhood should define our practice of surrogacy, surrogacy itself challenges and shifts our conceptions of motherhood. As we increasingly accept this practice, which is by nature governed by the economic relationship between the fertility industry and its wealthy clients, our respect for the "work," rights, and dignity of the surrogates themselves naturally declines. The commercial exchange inherent to surrogacy results in commodification of the children being bought and of the women who incubate them. Market language, by necessity, dominates surrogate contracts as lawyers increasingly try to protect their wealthy baby-seeking clients from blunders of the past. In contrast to the protections afforded for birth mothers who change their minds in the process of adoption, most surrogates agree to relinquish custody of their future children prior to their conception.

Other difficult situations are covered by these contracts as well. What happens, for example, when too many embryos successfully implant? Who gets to decide whether and which embryos are aborted for "selective reduction" to make the pregnancy "safer" for the remaining embryo(s)? What about when the product is "defective," found to be with a chromosomal abnormality such as Down syndrome? These contracts spell out, in no uncertain terms, that decisions about the continued existence of the growing child belong solely to the intended parents.

Generally, the right to cancel the order remains with the party who places the order. Any "my body, my choice" rhetoric ends the moment a surrogate's pen hits the paper. Never mind that pregnancy may have unexpected complications, or that pregnancy serves to form significant maternal bonds that change a woman's hormones and brain at a cellular level, or that forcing her to abort a subpar product may have lifelong consequences for her own fertility and mental health. Despite this total surrender of bodily autonomy, a surrogate may remain financially liable for the medical expenses incurred by her pregnancy and delivery, as have many surrogates who have been abandoned by the intended parents at some point during the process.[15] Whether due to a financial reversal, divorce of the intended couple, or an unexpected medical condition of the child, surrogates have been left carrying a child that has already effectively been orphaned.[16] The laws governing surrogacy vary worldwide, and not all contracts may be quite this dire, but the lopsided power dynamics of surrogacy are such that economic and legal factors are predominantly set to favor the buyer.

The ill effects of these all-too-common worst-case scenarios are heightened when one considers that the population of surrogates consists almost entirely of women who are, willingly or not, being exploited for their reproductive prowess. Nearly all surrogates receive compensation of some sort, ranging from $10,000 to upward of $100,000 (though it is the fertility industry that rakes in large sums for overseeing the process); even in so-called altruistic surrogacy, it is common for money to change hands as "reimbursement" for the inconveniences of pregnancy. And while every pregnancy comes with some degree of risk, surrogate pregnancy is riskier. Surrogates face increased risk of life-threatening complications like pre-eclampsia, and their children face higher risks of stillbirth, low birth weight, and long-term psychological difficulties.[17]

This is hardly an undertaking a woman agrees to lightly, or purely altruistically, without perceived significant benefit. By and large, women become surrogates for the money. While money is often not the only reason, the fact remains that, in the absence of compensation, very few women are willing to serve as surrogates. As Jennifer Lahl, President of the Center for Bioethics and Culture, observes, "It is a myth that surrogates are motivated by altruism. ... If you take away the money ... all these women who say they love to help build families ... overwhelmingly they go away when they're not being paid."[18] Most commercial services that also provide altruistic fulfillment to those who offer them, such as nursing, teaching, and fire-fighting, also disappear when money is no longer in the picture.

In the UK, where only altruistic surrogacy is permitted, only 0.2 percent of babies born through assisted reproduction are born via surrogacy.[19] That the exchange of money creates systemic exploitation is undeniable. Thankfully, the governments of some of the countries with populations most vulnerable to such exploitation have created legislation to protect their citizens. While developing countries initially emerged as popular centers for "reproductive tourism," many of them have moved to ban commercial surrogacy. After less than fourteen years, India shut down its booming "reproductive tourism" industry to protect its citizens from exploitation by Western foreigners seeking surrogates to grow their babies.[20] The conditions for surrogates there were particularly egregious, with the industry maintaining tight control of its surrogates by housing them for the entire term of their pregnancies in order to strictly monitor their diet and activities — all to ensure the best product.[21]

Some argue that commercial surrogacy is only *apparently* exploitative. In fact, they say, it is a good way to expand options for women of limited means, allowing single mothers to remain home with their children while earning a living, for example. They claim that the fact that surrogacy is exploitative and dehumanizing under some conditions does not rule out the possibility of introducing regulations to uphold the dignity of surrogates, thereby preserving the option. After all, it is the surrogates' choice to do with their bodies as they wish. If they wish to earn income by renting their wombs, who are we to restrict their reproductive freedom? This is the same argument made in favor of sex work, and indeed many have likened surrogacy to a kind of reproductive prostitution. It is also the argument made for the sale of kidneys and other non-essential organs. Who are we to limit what someone wishes to do with his own body?

Who we are is the human community. We are families, governments, and citizens with a vested interest in the kind of society we are becoming. And we *do* set limits for one another on what we can do with our own bodies. Most basically, those limits exist where our own bodies end and the bodies of others begin (except, curiously, in the case of abortion). We are not free to use our bodies to harm others. We are not even free to harm ourselves in many cases: We outlaw the use of certain substances and restrain the suicidal in psychiatric care (for now). Just laws uphold the freedom and dignity that properly belong to human persons. I argue that the relationship of motherhood, including the bodily integrity of motherhood, belongs among such sacred things: The unfolding of nascent human life is as inviolable as any sacred human good and thus warrants our protection.

The Effects of "Outsourcing" Pregnancy

Additionally, there is the question of what effects this "outsourcing" of pregnancy might have on parents approaching parenthood with the selectiveness of a consumer at the market rather than the wonder of a creature before his Creator. The posture of one ordering goods specifically to his liking is radically different from that of one who receives a long-awaited gift. The degree to which we experience gratitude and practice acceptance for whatever we find in the package we receive shifts wildly. Pregnancy and its trials often form a sort of boot camp of virtue, primarily for the woman but also for her husband, who must accompany her through the physical and emotional tolls of the nine liminal months in which they prepare for their roles as parents. The many sacrifices, large and small, required by pregnancy prepare them for the demands of parenthood, the continual dying to self in the sleepless nights to come. When conception is sought after and waited for, the time spent in anticipation creates the space for future parents to develop a posture of gratitude. Even in adoption, when the trials tend to be more emotional than those of physical pregnancy and labor, these hurdles serve to heighten parents' awareness of just how precious this gift of a child really is.

This is not to say that those who become parents via surrogacy do not value their children (on the contrary, we know precisely how much they value them monetarily). These reflections are not intended to be criticisms of parents who have chosen surrogacy, nor to question their affection for their children, but to examine the *processes* of these varying paths to parenthood as well as the influences those paths have on our growth in virtue and our attitudes toward our children. In these respects, not all paths are created equal. "Donation" and surrogacy lead us to view children as market goods and increasingly as products to be ordered to specification. When we regard them as such, intentionally or not, we jeopardize their freedom to unfold as persons in their own right. This leads to a child and, in turn, a society reshaped in the image held by parents who choose to make use of this practice. A path that requires that we dismember and devalue motherhood (or, at the very least, aspects of it), commodify our children, and lessen the dignity of both is a precarious path indeed.

Our societal emphases on consumerism and control unfortunately lead us to feel entitled to what some of us have and others have not been given. What is it about fertility that makes us believe we can lay claim to its fruits in this way? Some feminists, such as Gena Correa, argue that the fertility industry, the *pharmacracy*, is men's attempt to wrest control of female fertility and place it firmly in men's domain.[22] The fertility industry now caters to (or preys upon) infertile couples, same-sex couples, and single people (gay and straight alike) who find themselves unable (or unwilling) to procreate naturally. This is an industry that could only arise in a society that feels entitled to grasp at what belongs to someone else — her fertility, her womb, her future children.

In our eagerness to grasp at what we feel ought to be ours by right (see chapter 1), we are willing to snatch at things that are sacred. If we maintained awe and reverence for womanhood and its capacity (with its natural limits) for motherhood, we would know that this is an area where we ought to "remove the sandals "; the begetting of life is holy ground (see Ex 3:5). Eggs and sperm are unlike kidneys. What is given is not merely a nonvital bit of self. If it does what it is intended to do, it participates in the creation of one's biological child.

Pregnancy is not, as the abortionists would have us believe, merely the incubation of an embryo. It is the foundation of the maternal relationship. Motherhood begins at conception. Any attempt to sever pregnancy from motherhood is nonsensical; at no other point is a child so dependent on its mother, or a mother's existence so wholly subject to her child. It is a physical reality. A father's ability to be in unmediated relationship with his child begins at birth; a mother begins caring for her child at conception. The fracturing of motherhood into its component parts, the delegation of the difficult or disdainful aspects of it — these are actions that are redefining the most basic of human relationships. For more on how the widespread use of reproductive technologies is transforming the human community, see chapter 11.

The Baby Market

The fertility industry offers a shiny promise: We can sell you that which God has not given. It is not in the business of restoration of health, which is simpler but not nearly as profitable or prestigious. Instead, the industry creates children to be bought and sold according to the specifications of the buyer. Women's bodies are rented via contracts that occasionally include their future children (gametes) in the price of sale. And it is indeed a *sale*. The sums of money that change hands are too large to represent anything other than a market transaction, the risks ignored too great to be attributed to altruism.

If we forbid the selling of organs to prevent the ill of coercion, why do we not forbid the selling of one's future children? If the reason for organ donation (prevention of the recipient's death) isn't enough to warrant legalization of the sale of organs, how do we justify selling gametes to those who merely (by comparison) desire children? With the risks of egg "donation" and surrogacy commensurate with those of organ donation, what can account for the continued permissibility of this practice but a perverted view of freedom and deep, dark pockets?

Some argue that the physical link between donors (biological parents) and their children ought to be disregarded, and that, aside from any pertinent health information, the genetic link is of little consequence. This argument is narrowly one-sided. If it is indeed true that the genetics are of little consequence, then why the need for surrogacy or gamete "donation" at all? (Adoption is the obvious solution if genetic relationship doesn't matter.) Why the lawsuits and outrage when some, such as Dr. Barwin, inseminate using incorrect (or even their own) sperm? Was the goal not conception? The buyers got what they paid for: a child. As demonstrated by the multimillion-dollar lawsuit against Dr. Barwin, biology is of great value to intended parents. So why does the biology of the "donor" carry so little weight that his moral responsibility to his child(ren) is so easily signed away? When a man "donates" his sperm via a one-night stand, his responsibilities are written into law and come with a monthly price tag. If we take biological parenthood seriously enough to attach nearly twenty years of fiscal responsibility for an unintended conception, how do we justify the conception of biological children for intentional abandonment?

If the genetic link does not matter, then it should be unconscionable to think of spending exorbitant amounts of money to have a child produced rather than rescuing one of the millions of orphans waiting for adoption — over 100,000 in America and 20 million worldwide.[23] These are living, breathing children who lack the love and support of families. It points to our understanding of children as private property that we bear such little sense of communal responsibility for these children that we would seek to commission the creation of new children in order to procure "our own."

Perhaps adoption is less palatable to us because it appears more complex and is a process over which we have less control. Existing children come with baggage. Adoption is legally complicated, time-consuming, and often disappointing in its failure to secure the desired child — hurdles that don't exist with safe, straightforward, and effective fertility factories.

But the red tape and legal requirements faced by families desperate to adopt exist in large part for the protection of the children. Children who are produced, on the other hand, usually have no legal protections whatsoever

as they are delivered to their new parents. As long as potential parents (if indeed that is what these child-seeking
persons intend to become) have cash in hand, they can
purchase a future child with little inquiry into their motives. They might face legal challenges if they are *caught* in
ill treatment of the child for which they paid good money,
but until that time, the product they have commissioned
is their own possession to abuse, traffic, or pornographize
at will. This is a situation that could be exploited by child
traffickers in states like New York, which have no residen-
cy requirement.

Why is it that we are willing to keep children in less-
than-ideal foster and other arrangements for their own
protection from potential adoptive parents with less than
pure motives, but we do not worry about those who are
hiring women and doctors to create children on their behalf? Is it that we place greater faith in the character of
those whose socioeconomic status affords them the freedom to pursue surrogacy?

This path is one that inevitably leads to children being
made to order (indeed, the technology of gene editing is
already available and affordable, with no existing US laws
to govern private research on its use — more on that in
chapter 11).[24] Children will be made to suit the whims of
the wealthy, who may prize traits undesirable to the population at large — perhaps even undesirable to the children
themselves.

A Communal Responsibility

As we proceed as a human community, we have a grave responsibility to ourselves, our children, and future generations to promote practices that further the common good, and to prohibit those which obscure it. We need to ask difficult questions, and *if* we choose to proceed at all, we must do so with caution. Some questions we might ask along the way include the following: Does this practice lend itself to love? Surely for the future parents and their intended children. But what about for the biological and gestational mothers? What about for the siblings and grandparents and cousins of those who have been given away? What kind of virtues or vices do these practices foster within us? What kind of society do they help to create? What are the respective burdens and benefits of these practices? Who bears and receives each? Weighed against one another, how do they stack up?

Reluctant as we Americans tend to be in acknowledging our interdependence, we cannot continue to thrust our heads in the sand and pretend that the satisfaction of each person's desires has no effect on the kind of society we create. Our choices do not exist in isolation; they have consequences for us all. Together we proceed like a ship, steering by degrees, and once we catch sight of disaster, it may be too late to change course.

Can we turn society away from pursuing absolute individual autonomy and recover focus on the communal aspects of human life?

CHAPTER 11

Brave New World

Is it ethical to alter the genetic makeup of children? Should we create children with three parents? What about creating sperm from female stem cells, to the end of creating a child with two biological mothers? Is it ethical to incubate a growing baby in an artificial womb? Could a womb like that end the perceived need for abortion? These kinds of questions might seem like science fiction, and indeed they were when Aldous Huxley, an agnostic, published his dystopian novel *Brave New World* nearly one hundred years ago. Huxley weaved a fictitious world in which progeny were designed and grown in laboratories, children were raised by the state rather than in families, promiscuity was encouraged and monogamy considered grotesque, and the government endorsed self-medication with a "harmless" drug that kept its users in a placated state. All things considered, one has to wonder if Huxley wasn't more a prophet than a novelist.

Technological Dystopia

Likewise, C. S. Lewis, a Christian convert and contemporary of Huxley, saw the writing on the wall. In *The Abolition of Man,* he foretold the progression of society's preoccupation with mastery of nature. An increasingly scientific and technological worldview that denigrates the role of religion, morality, and character leaves little room for questions about who we become through the kinds of interventions we employ. Lewis saw that the ultimate fruit of moral subjectivism was a world in which there was less freedom, not more, as the technological capabilities to alter man's nature would ultimately belong to whoever amassed the most power and therefore the ability to use it however he wished:

> The final stage is come when Man by eugenics, by pre-natal conditioning, and by an education and propaganda based on a perfect applied psychology, has obtained full control over himself. *Human nature will be the last part of Nature to surrender to Man.*[1]

The explosion of new technologies and applications is truly exciting, but with this exciting potential comes the responsibility to reflect on its meaning for the human community. We must refrain from rushing down an un-examined path. Medicine in general and reproductive medicine in particular are coming to be defined not as the restoration of human health, but as the optimization of human well-being. No longer are the goals of medicine strictly "medical." Researchers pursue drugs for cognitive and physical enhancements that not only improve our functioning on the bell curve but seek also to redefine the curve entirely.

As we continue to expand the umbrella of medicine, we are slowly but surely redefining what it means to be human. We have reached an era in which we cannot af-ford the naïvety of believing that science and medicine are value-neutral; they will always be tools subject to the val-ues of those who wield them. We can no longer afford to leave the morality of new technologies and procedures to the discernment of those fascinated by their possibility or to those who may reap economic or therapeutic benefits from them. These procedures increasingly shape not only the individuals who employ them, but also future genera-tions of humanity.

There is more than the autonomous will at stake here, and as a human community we must weigh in on these questions. Which of these technologies enhance our hu-manity, and which detract from it? Medical advances hap-pen quickly, often pushed ahead by the Machiavellian will to achieve new discoveries or generate immense profits. Unbelievable though it may be, the imaginings of science fiction are on the cusp of becoming our reality. Some already have. We need to advance our discussions ahead of our capabilities. It is much easier to encourage caution and thoughtful discussion about a possibility than it is to reverse the tide once that possibility becomes commonplace, having been uncritically embedded into the fabric of our society. That is the subject of this chapter: What procedures are on the table for debate as advances on the horizon, and what is our response to them as thoughtful people of faith?

Catholic Scholarship, Christian Imagination

Because the emerging technologies discussed in this chapter are new and developments rapidly occurring, there is little magisterial teaching that addresses them directly beyond what we have already discussed in chapter 10. The National Catholic Bioethics Center (ncbcenter.org) offers resources such as courses, newsletters, and other publications. The Center is a wealth of the most current Catholic scholarship and thought on emerging medical technologies and treatments. The work of these scholars, theologians, and ethicists consists of applying the ancient wisdom of the Church to the new quandaries we encounter. Although it by no means represents "the" Catholic position on issues on which the Magisterium has not yet ruled, it contributes in many ways to the ongoing development of what may one day become those teachings. Likewise, the Pontifical Academy for Life exists to conduct bioethical research on these types of issues in relation to magisterial teachings.

While many of these developments might set off our dystopian warning bells, casting dark and gloomy shadows on the future of our moral landscape, the Christian imagination offers us a brighter light through which to view them. As I have previously reflected:

> The Resurrection is not a pithy consolation prize or distant symbol of hope to be realized only at the end of the Christian life. The reality that Christ has conquered death and lives in us is a *present* reality. We can bemoan the signs of the times with heavy hearts, and there is much in our society to lament, but our call is to be an Easter people, as Pope John Paul II reminded us in the midst of the Cold War:
>
>> We do not pretend that life is all beauty. We are aware of darkness and sin, of poverty and pain. But we know Jesus has conquered sin and passed through his own pain to the glory of the Resurrection. And we live in the light of his Paschal Mystery — the mystery of his Death and Resurrection. "We are an Easter People and Alleluia is our song!" We are not looking for a shallow joy but rather a joy that comes from faith, that grows through unselfish love, that respects the "fundamental duty of love of neighbour, without which

it would be unbecoming to speak of Joy." We realize that joy is demanding; it demands unselfishness; it demands a readiness to say with Mary: "Be it done unto me according to thy word."

The state of our world is not something to bemoan or escape from; it is the ground on which our own *Fiat* takes form. The Almighty Creator of the universe has chosen and called each of us to serve Him in these particular circumstances. The world we live in is begging for our prophetic response.[2]

The New(est) Eugenics

Along with the decline in reverence for God has come a lost sense of the sanctity and dignity of the human person. How can that which is merely matter be sacred? How can we speak of "violating" the purely mechanical? As Lewis so presciently grasped, the attempt to wield ultimate control over the material aspects of nature has given us the impression that we both can and ought to control all aspects of our own nature. The more we use technologies that give us access to control over who we are and what kinds of children we bear, the more we will exercise that control. It seems we can't help ourselves.

What's left after we decide to employ these technologies is to decide *how*. Lewis recognized that the exercise of these technologies would eventually become an exercise of power over the weak: "What we call Man's power over Nature turns out to be a power exercised by some men over other men with Nature as its instrument."[3] In our fervor to eliminate suffering, to improve ourselves — indeed, to purify ourselves — it is inevitable that the eugenic impulses of the early twentieth century are once again rising (if they ever truly left). American campaigns for mass sterilizations of the "unfit" (ranging from the mentally and physically disabled, to the criminally minded, to those who were merely the wrong race) faded into the background following the horrors of the Second World War. While the push for mass sterilizations has quieted, one eugenic tool has only increased in popularity and use: Contraception has, from the outset, been employed for eugenic purposes; Margaret Sanger, founder of Planned Parenthood, was an avid supporter of eugenics and wrote often of the potential of contraception to curb the growth of the Black population.[4] And since the early 1980s, doctors have employed amniocentesis and other prenatal testing techniques in conjunction with abortion to prevent the births of individuals with Down syndrome and other genetic conditions, as discussed in chapter 5.

We are on the brink of a return to more aggressive forms of eugenic control. British courts backed a mother's decision to euthanize her twelve-year-old disabled daughter,[5] and current legislation in Belgium and the Netherlands allows parents to euthanize their terminally ill children.[6] Academics attempt to justify the practice of "after-birth abortion" — that is, infanticide for children

up to age two.[7] The invention of the genetic editing technique CRISPR and the sequencing of the human genome
in recent years have shifted "designer babies" from the
category of science fiction to imminent reality. Genetically
altered babies have already been born in China.[8]

Once we remove God and human dignity from the
equation, all that remains to adjudicate decisions on these
matters is power. As Lewis comments, "If any one age really attains [as our age has], by eugenics and scientific education, the power to make its descendants what it pleases,
all men who live after it are the patients of that power."[9]
Who gets to decide which lives are worth protecting, and
on what basis? The more we relegate any and all forms of
weakness and vulnerability to the realm of the unacceptable, the less room there is for *any* form of imperfection.
The fewer individuals there are in vulnerable situations,
the less we as a community are alerted to their needs. In
eliminating those populations with disabilities, we lessen
our collective compassion. When we refuse to care for the
vulnerable, we become less human, not more so. Each of
us is born helpless (those of us who are lucky enough to be
permitted to be born). If anything in us needs stamping
out, it is not our weakness or dependence, but our tendency to despise such humanizing qualities to the point of destruction.

Unintended Genetic Ramifications
A negative consequence of widespread sperm donation
and artificial insemination already manifesting itself is

narrowed genetic selection for future generations. We have seen cases of hundreds of children being born of the same father.[10] Too much genetic similarity in successive generations jeopardizes our biodiversity. Recognizing this risk, the American Society for Reproductive Medicine (ASRM) suggests limiting donors to twenty-five live births per population area of 800,000 to control for that effect.[11]

And playing with our genetics comes with other unintended consequences. Although we have the capability to map the human genome, we are far from understanding the intricate ways in which it works. This is true of even basic characteristics; the same genotype can vary widely in its manifestations (phenotypes). It is even truer as we attempt to select for specific personality traits. Genetic "code" is a misnomer in that it is not as straightforward as computer code, where the language is precise and the relationship between input and output is clear. In the field of genetics, each gene is influenced not only by our environment, but also by the constellation of genes that together make up the code. When we select a certain characteristic, we also inadvertently choose the constellation of traits associated with it. It's likely that some traits our society deems desirable are associated with other, less desirable traits. Imagine the "scatterbrained genius" or very assertive risk-taker. In one instance, a sperm donor for the "genius" sperm bank Xytex failed to disclose his schizophrenia at the time of his "donations."[12] The thirty-six sets of parents who selected his genes for their children did so because of his intelligence; they were not prepared for the risk of mental illness written into that same code.

Even those without religious faith can recognize that when it comes to designing our progeny, "playing God" is playing with fire. Whether we see ourselves surrendering that power to natural selection, random chance, or God Himself, we stand to fare far better taking an approach of humility. The realm of what we do not know necessarily remains opaque and inaccessible to us; no matter how much of this territory we manage to wrestle into that which we have conquered, we will never know how much remains outside our domain. Tinkering with our genetics unleashes our laboratory experiments into the wild for all of humanity to become the test field. It will not matter who has opted "in" when none of us has the choice to opt "out."

Coming Soon: Mechanical Wombs, Artificial Gametes, and Cloning

As we explore continually emerging technologies, it is imperative that we stop and consider the societal as well as medical implications of their use. We cannot intervene in the human body without touching the human person; as we saw in chapter 10, the manipulation of our bodies alters our relationships and restructures how we function as a society. Among these emerging technologies are artificial wombs,[13] to which thinkers have attributed the potential ability both to end abortion (by allowing the transfer of fetuses from wombs where they are not welcome into waiting incubators)[14] and to become the means of creating the baby factories of Huxley's repugnant new world.[15] How ought we navigate the use of mechanical uteruses? On the one hand, how wonderful it would be to extend our existing technology to support prematurely born infants by moving viability to as young an age as possible. On the other hand, it may be quite arrogant to assume that we can replicate with mechanical parts all the essential aspects of the physical care of a mother's womb. Evidence regarding the effects of physical touch[16] and reading aloud[17] to infants suggests that these human interactions have huge impacts on their development. Likely such interactions are similarly impactful prior to birth. We don't know the effects of a mother's voice, touch, and hormones on a prenatal infant's body and mind. Will we truly subject future human beings to this kind of radical experimentation in order to find out?

A further way in which researchers are seeking to control reproduction is through the creation of artificial gametes. Adult stem cells from female mice can be coaxed into becoming sperm and used to fertilize an egg, resulting in mice created using artificial gametes.[18] Researchers have also successfully produced human sperm and eggs.[19] It is only a matter of time and funding before these artificial gametes are employed in the production of a live human embryo. Theoretically, this means that an embryo could eventually be conceived as the genetic child of two women. This has implications for same-sex couples, who until now have had to make use of donor gametes to reproduce. The conversation is already framed in terms of rights, the right to reproduce being the assumed basis for same-sex couples to pursue IVF. Should we allow this? Are we willing to further dispense with the unique contributions of fatherhood or motherhood to the well-being of our children to satisfy the desires of the parents who will raise them?

What do we make of our ability to create children with three (or more) parents, editing out defective DNA and introducing additional genetic parents?[20] May we reproduce via cloning? We have the technology; researchers have successfully created cloned embryos from both embryos and living adults (although no attempt has yet been made to gestate or birth human clones).[21] May we clone whomever we wish? If someone wanted to raise a child genetically identical to, say, Kobe Bryant or Britney Spears, who should determine whether he had the right to do so? May we create a clone of a sick child to provide genetically identical organs?

Redefining Humanity

These are not scientific or medical questions. These technologies and procedures raise ethical and relational questions that force us to examine our previously held notions of who we are as human beings. Some might argue that these manipulations are simply the next step in our evolution. Yet among the greatest of our current capabilities is the ability to reason. We can reflect and deliberate and make choices. Whatever capabilities we might be able to manage to manufacture into ourselves, we must acknowledge that there is no way we can know in advance what effects our tampering will have. We are, voluntarily or not, becoming the subjects of a population-wide research project, the results of which will span generations.

The technologies may be new, but they have us circling back to revisit ancient questions: What does it mean to be human? What is the good life? What do we owe one another? In many ways, these ends we are pursuing, remarkable feats of scientific achievement as they may be, represent the easy way out. Just as the fitness industry capitalizes on our unwillingness to put in the effort required to achieve hard goals, so too will industries use these new technologies to offer the promise of making us "better." But are these goals — perfect health, enhanced intelligence, unsurpassed talent — ends truly worth pursuing? Does individual transhuman capability really represent what is powerfully compelling about the human spirit? Do these interventions make us more loving or virtuous? What good will it do us to gain the world if it comes at the cost of our souls?

If we ask ourselves who the truly great human beings are, I suspect our answers will not be those who possessed monumental abilities. Although we marvel at the creativity of Michelangelo, the literary prowess of Shakespeare, the revolutionary mind of Einstein, in the end it is not remarkable achievements that make one great at *being human*. Instead, I like to think that people like St. Teresa of Calcutta, Mahatma Gandhi, and Dr. Martin Luther King Jr. would come to our minds. Such remarkable love, self-sacrifice, and service to our fellow man are the real measure of our humanity. Those who act in such love represent the Christian ideal, and the beautiful thing about it is that none of us need be well endowed with any capability to begin. Following the Little Way of Saint Thérèse, each of us can do small things with great love. The Christian ideal is Christ, and if He offers us any list of characteristics worth pursuing, it is the Beatitudes. "Blessed are the poor," "the meek," "those who hunger and thirst for righteousness," "the merciful," "the pure in heart," "the peacemakers,"(Mt 5:3–9) — these are not attributes we can take a pill or alter a gene to produce. We cannot surgically remove the vice germinating in our hearts. We have to do some heavy lifting. We have to act.

The best of us will not be found by narrowing and selecting specific capabilities. The elimination of suffering will not produce joy. If we seek to be truly free, we must acknowledge our responsibilities to one another. As a society, we will flourish to the extent that we all can flourish individually. Fr. Greg Boyle describes this process as widening the circle of compassion:

Imagine no one standing outside of that circle, moving ourselves closer to the margins so that the margins themselves will be erased. We stand there with those whose dignity has been denied. We locate ourselves with the poor and the powerless and the voiceless. At the edges, we join the easily despised and the readily left out. We stand with the demonized so that the demonizing will stop. We situate ourselves right next to the disposable so that the day will come when we stop throwing people away.[22]

As we imagine making ourselves and society "better," we need to conceive not of an earthly perfection, but a glorified one. Compassion, after all, means suffering with another, and all real love requires sacrifice. If we aim for the elimination of suffering and the creation of invulnerable beings, what chance does such a society stand of learning to rely on one another and patiently bear wrongs? In a population of specimens with homogeneously high IQs and perfect health, how many will develop the heart of Saint Teresa? Much more likely is an outcome in which every man becomes an island in a vast sea of isolation.

From our incomplete Tower of Babel to the apostles' squabbles over who deserved the best seat in the kingdom of heaven, the impulse toward perfection seems a part of human nature. Yet, as Jesus Himself reminds us, real greatness lies not in becoming the pinnacle of anything, but in lowliness: "Whoever wishes to be great among you must be your servant, and whoever wishes to be first among you must be your slave" (Mt 20:26–27). And let's not forget that first among us, our "tainted nature's solitary boast,"[23] is a woman, a mother, whose humility and docility opened the way to salvation for us all. In emptying herself, this simple woman from Nazareth allowed herself to be filled with grace. Let us pray, then, that whatever humanity might become through the technologies we choose to employ, we preserve the freedom to become empty so that the Holy Spirit may animate us, and the will to lay down our lives for those whom we love.

CHAPTER 12

Spiritual Motherhood: A Prophetic Calling

Motherhood is the epitome of womanhood, a profound call that echoes in the heart of every woman. As Alice von Hildebrand explains, "A woman by her very nature is maternal — for every woman, whether married or unmarried, is called upon to be a biological, psychological, or spiritual mother — she knows intuitively that to give, to nurture, to care for others, to suffer with and for them — for maternity implies suffering — is infinitely more valuable in God's sight than to conquer nations and fly to the moon."[1]

Worth noting is that the Church speaks of herself in feminine terms. She is the Bride of Christ, recipient of

His salvific sacrifice, endowed with the sacred responsibility to safeguard and proclaim His teachings. Pope St.
John XXIII refers to her as *Mater et Magistra* (Mother and
Teacher) in his 1961 document of the same name,[2] for example, as does Pope St. John Paul II in *Familiaris Consortio* when discussing the Church's moral authority.[3] While
many are quick to criticize the Church as patriarchal and
oppressive in its moral rigidity, this document clearly
identifies her instructive role as a distinctly maternal one.
Rather than resent the Church's moral guidance, we are
to regard it as akin to maternal correction. Likewise, then,
as women, we exercise the faculty of maternal correction
as an extension of our prophetic call; "admonishing the
sinner" is a spiritual act of mercy.

However, we live in an age that regards the identifica-
tion of sin as the worst of all sins. Even within Christian
circles, it is common to hear the phrases "Don't judge" or
"I'm not judging." So afraid are we to commit this trans-
gression called judgment that we hesitate to call out even
the most blatant of wrongs. This means that, as women
called to spiritual motherhood, we are afraid to live out a
central part of our identity. When we allow fear to eclipse
our responsibilities to admonish grave wrongs and encourage virtue over vice, we abandon a core duty of our
common call to spiritual motherhood. Although instruct-
ing the ignorant and admonishing the sinner are spiritual
works of mercy that women are especially gifted at carrying out with all the necessary compassion, we seem to have
abandoned this role in our modern age due to a misguided

notion that it harms rather than helps our neighbor.

While it is true that puritanical attitudes have historically led to overemphasis on shame, particularly here in America, the antidote is not to deny the reality of sin altogether. Virtue is found at the midpoint of two extremes. It is our duty as Christians, as spiritual mothers, to care for the spiritual health of our society by speaking the truth about practices that do not uphold human dignity. In this way, we shelter and protect those around us who may be unable to recognize these threats, much less defend themselves. If we saw a child run out into the street, we would call out to stop her. We might even go out into the street ourselves and lead that child by the hand back to safety. We would not watch idly as she wandered into the path of an oncoming vehicle, making claims about protecting her autonomy or out of fear we might offend her mother by imposing our own parenting strategy.

My husband and I lost track of our daughter in a hardware store when she was about two years old. Another woman, a mother herself, found our daughter and guided her to the counter. "I found her talking to the tile," she said with a laugh, but of course I couldn't laugh. I could barely speak through the tears of relief running down my face. What if the woman had passed that moment by? "It's not for me to judge how other people parent," she might have told herself. A far darker fate might have awaited my child. This woman saw a child in a precarious situation, recognized her own moral responsibility to that child, and took action. Thank God she did not shy away because it "wa~

her place." If only we could recognize more clearly the perilous situations in which so many of those close to us find their souls. Rather than concern for propriety or minding our own business, we might remember our responsibility to and for our loved ones and our broader human community.

Making Space for Moral Judgment

Moral judgment didn't use to be a social faux pas. It used to be a virtue. We called it prudence: the art of practical wisdom. When we divorce our minds from the realities of objective truth and goodness, what remains is merely the subjective will of each individual. A society like this has no use or room for moral discourse. There is nothing left for a community to do except refrain from each "imposing" his will on the other.

In taking a hands-off approach to the moral quandaries that new technologies and forms of reproduction present, we are abdicating our responsibility to one another. We are watching our society, our coworkers, our friends and family, spiritually suffocate and treating it as though they've merely chosen a different entree at the buffet line. "We all like different things," my four-year-old is fond of saying — and at preschool, where they're bickering over whether to play in the rice bin or paste Cheerios™ on construction paper, this is an appropriate attitude to cultivate. When we enter the realm of those choices that change the trajectory of our eternal souls, however, the stakes are quite a bit higher. The choice is not between meals that differ by degrees of taste or nutritional value; the difference is between food that nourishes and things that may not only fail to satisfy us, but actually poison us at varying rates.

The response required is not to put down this book and immediately begin barking orders. Whether dealing with a picky toddler or a rebellious teenager, the quickest way to close their mouths or minds is to attempt to fill them by force. And so it is with spiritual motherhood: always, we are called to witness and to invitation. This can be frustrating and even heartbreaking. It is difficult to navigate, and we might lose friendships regardless of how kindly we communicate our hopes for one another to make life-giving, dignity-affirming choices. There will be times when our only recourse is prayer.

We need something of a renaissance, or perhaps just a reality check, in the way we view engaging one another in dialogue. Dialogue is not dangerous; the idea that we need to designate spaces as "shelter" from unpalatable ideas is insulting. We are not corseted Victorians likely to swoon when confronted with a proposal that offends our delicate sensibilities. It *can* be difficult to navigate tense conversations about differing points of view, and this difficulty does increase when the subject is sensitive. Stakes rise even higher when the context is conversation with a loved one rather than dispassionate academic discourse. But however difficult dialogue may be, we are *capable*.

God has entrusted this spiritual work of mercy — fraternal correction — to women in a special way. As the elders in Julie Otsuka's novel *The Buddha in the Attic* echo,

"Women are weak, but mothers are strong."[4] The strength in these echoes is that which St. Francis de Sales is widely attributed to have identified: "There is nothing so strong as true gentleness, and nothing so gentle as true strength." We know we have lost our sense of this quality in motherhood when we view the Church's guidance as authoritarian, domineering, or paternalistic. *She*, the Church, the bride of Christ, is *mother* to her members, and her guidance to us rises out of her compassion. In our adolescent preoccupation with control, we tend to view any and all dictates in a restrictive light. The moral guidance the Church offers us is entirely different. Her compassionate correction issues out of *hesed*: mercy. This loving-kindness, as the Hebrew is sometimes translated, is the compassion of Jesus, whose heart was moved when He saw crowds of people, "like sheep without a shepherd" (Mt 9:36). *This* is the direction the Church offers us, the mercy of a Good Shepherd willing to lay down his life for the rescue of sheep who insist on straying among the wolves.

The Good News about Mercy

The truly tragic thing about the cultural moratorium on judgment is its ironic consequence of creating a vastly more judgmental world. The nonjudgment worldview holds that behavior is mostly OK, so long as it doesn't have negative consequences for other people. This has the result of absolving most of us from most of our sins, creating a class of basically good people. It separates this class from the unacceptable people: murderers, rapists, pedophiles, human traffickers, etc. Of course, we judge those actions as wrong, because we recognize the grave harms of those offenses. But what is behind the nonjudgment worldview is actually the opposite impetus to separate all people into these two classes: the basically good and the unacceptable. The emphasis on nonjudgment stems from the desire to create more space in this class of the basically good. This worldview rings of Puritanical influence: a heaven and hell with no in-between, the saved and damned. Although the criterion for salvation in Protestant theology is acceptance of Christ, we can see how the culture has evolved out of this dichotomous categorization of our souls. Secular culture has kept the impetus to judge and to separate; it has merely changed the measure.

The Catholic worldview is different; we hold that "all have sinned and fall short of the glory of God" (Rom 3:23). While this fallenness tarnishes each of us, it cannot diminish our innate dignity. We are all created in the image and likeness of God, and while we can mar that image through sin, it can never be lost. There are no separate classes of people. We recognize the dignity in the murderer, the unborn, the refugee, the rapist, the severely disabled — there is *no* disqualifying any human being from the realm of "us." There is no "them."

Do we embody that perfectly? Nope. We struggle. And here's the beautiful part: We have the freedom to recognize our struggles and our sinfulness, to repent, and to move on. It is precisely because we have the freedom to judge our collective actions that we are able to throw ourselves at the feet of Jesus and accept the sweet embrace of His mercy.

Spiritual Mothers Proclaim the Truth

By virtue of our baptism, all Christians are anointed in the roles of Christ: priest (prayer and sacrifice), prophet (proclaiming the truth), king (servant leadership). It is the middle role, that of prophet, which places squarely on our shoulders the responsibility to proclaim the Good News of Christ. And it is *good* news, no matter how inconvenient or unpopular, though honoring that Good News may require that we pass through moments and trials that feel anything but good. As Flannery O'Connor wrote:

> The truth does not change according to our ability to stomach it emotionally. A higher paradox confounds emotion as well as reason and there are long periods in the lives of all of us, and all of the saints, when the truth as revealed by faith is hideous, emotionally disturbing, downright repulsive.[5]

At times, being a truth-bearer calls us to refinement by fire, whether that means we bear the crucible of public scrutiny or even martyrdom.

But bear the truth in love we must. Our call to spiritual motherhood carries within it our call to be prophetic. When we shy away from opportunities to witness the truth in kindness, we shelter ourselves from challenge and rebuff. The price of hiding our convictions, however, is that we withhold the truth and, with it, the freedom Jesus has promised us. In declaring the truth, we run the risk of being crucified. History has not been kind to prophets and martyrs. But as we all must die, is this not a hill worth dying on?

It is time to reclaim our spiritual motherhood, to refuse to stand by and watch as our culture engages in exploitative practices that threaten to dehumanize us all. When it comes to altering the family, the basic structure upon which all of society is built, when it comes to reproduction and how we receive and raise our children, no "choice" remains individual. The choice of one impacts the nature of the community to which we all belong.

If our culture succeeds in sanitizing our discourse of moral values, of appeals to the good, all that will be left to govern our future is power. We cannot leave our future to the hands of whichever perspective manages to amass the most power — void of any criterion on which to judge the value of that viewpoint. So, let us own our spiritual motherhood and, with it, our right to denounce certain practices and promote others according to the criteria of love and goodness established by the Word of God. For the sake of individual souls as well as the future generations we will never know, we must refuse to be silent. We must raise our voices, however "unsafe" our echoes may resound in delicate ears. When they accuse us of judgment, let them. If we conduct ourselves in love and patiently bear these wrongs, our words carry all the more weight.

As Christ commanded, we shall "shake off the dust"

as we leave behind those who refuse to listen (see Mt 10:14). As Christ directed, we will turn the other cheek to those who strike us (Mt 5:39). As Christ did, we will lay down our lives for those who scoff at and spit upon us. These are tough expectations, but as Saint Peter himself declared, "Lord, to whom can we go? You have the words of eternal life" (Jn 6:68). And it is in following Christ's words and example that we discover the truth of who we are and reach the pinnacle of who we were made to be — not gods ourselves, as the ancient deception claims, but creatures, sons and daughters thoroughly conformed to God's will. And whom do we have as the perfect model of this radical obedience? The woman who thwarted Satan in her yes to motherhood. Let us reclaim our own yes to motherhood as we echo Mary's fearless words: "Let it be with me according to your word" (Lk 1:38).

Acknowledgments

This book would not exist without the support of so many people God put into my path during the writing and development process, not least of all every barista who artfully fueled my caffeine addiction. First, my husband, Garrett, whose witness brought me into the Catholic Church, whose love most clearly images God's for me, and who spent many a breath affirming the value of this work and reminding me to take a break when I wanted to throw it all in a lake. My children, simultaneously my greatest gifts and challenges, bring more meaning and joy to my life than any project I could dream up. I also thank God for the support of Caitlan Rangel, my dear friend, constant cheerleader, and inspiration in motherhood.

Many thanks are due to my editors Mary Beth Gilt-ner, who took a chance on developing this project with me, and Christina Nichols for her insights, scalpel-like precision with the text, and voracious demand for citations. I am indebted to Sam Povlock for the early opportunities to write on these topics and deeply grateful for the community she has built at FemCatholic. I must also thank Grace Emily Stark, whose research and suggestions were pivotal in shaping this book, and Dr. Christopher Kaczor, whose course inspired me to pursue bioethics, whose thought has been critical and foundational in shaping my own, and whose mentorship and encouragement has been priceless. I would also like to thank my professors Dr. Roberto Dell'Oro for teaching me to see the philosophical roots of ages both current and ancient, and Dr. Anna Harrison for taking the time to teach her students to write, to "sacrifice everything for clarity." For their work offering additional edits and feedback, I thank Catherine Sullivan, Theresa Williams, and Heather Blume.

And I must thank my parents, who introduced me to Jesus, put me through over a decade of Catholic school, and didn't bat an eye when I "threw it all away" to be home with my children — which is where my writing really began.

Guides for Discussion and Digging Deeper

Chapter 1: The Spiritual Roots of Our Madness

For Discussion

Where do you see the lies in the first column of the chart on page 26 manifest themselves in your own life or in our culture?

Which lie do you think presents the most pressing problem?

What is the most uplifting aspect of the Christian message as an antidote to the problems of our time?

Have you thought about morality as a path to true happiness before? How does this presentation of it resonate (or not) with your understanding?

What is one way you can challenge yourself to live the teachings of the Church more genuinely? Is it researching or praying about a teaching you disagree with? Reconciling with a loved one? Name one concrete action you can take this week.

Digging Deeper

BOOKS

Paul Waddell, *Happiness and the Christian Moral Life: An Introduction to Christian Ethics.* Lanham, MD: Rowman & Littlefield, 2007.

Matt Walsh, *The Unholy Trinity: Blocking the Left's Assault on Life, Marriage, and Gender.* New York: The Crown Publishing Group, 2017.

VIDEOS

Bishop Robert Barron, "Catholic Morality 101." YouTube, 2020.

Bishop Robert Barron, "Ideas Have Consequences: The Philosophers Who Shaped the 20th Century." YouTube, 2020.

Fr. Robert Spitzer, Four Levels of Happiness™. YouTube, 2017.

Chapter 2: Male and Female He Created Them

For Discussion

What are some of the unique gifts of men and women? What makes these more than mere stereotypes?

How has feminism made the world better for women? What are its drawbacks?

What are some of the gifts of the feminine genius in a family? In the workplace? In government?

What is one "feminine" quality that you struggle to value? Why do you think that is?

Why do children need both a mother and a father? What are some ways you've seen families make it work when this is no longer an option?

Digging Deeper

BOOKS

Ryan T. Anderson, *When Harry Became Sally: Responding to the Transgender Movement*. New York: Encounter Books, 2017.

Sue Browder, *Subverted: How I Helped the Women's Movement Hijack the Sexual Revolution*. San

Francisco: Ignatius Press, 2019.

Kimberly Cook, *Motherhood Redeemed: How Radical Feminism Betrayed Maternal Love.* Charlotte, NC: TAN Books, 2020.

Abigail Favale, *The Genesis of Gender: A Christian Theory.* San Francisco: Ignatius Press, 2022.

Carrie Gress, *The Anti-Mary Exposed: Rescuing the Culture from Toxic Femininity.* Charlotte, NC: TAN Books, 2019.

Leah Jacobson, *Wholistic Feminism: Healing the Identity Crisis Caused by the Women's Movement.* Ironton, MN: Lumen Press, 2021.

Pope St. John Paul II, *Man and Women He Created Them.* Boston: Pauline Books and Media, 2006.

Ashley McGuire, *Sex Scandal: The Drive to Abolish Male and Female.* Washington, DC: Regnery Publishing, 2017.

Rebekah Merkle, *Eve in Exile: The Restoration of Femininity.* Moscow, ID: Cannon Press, 2016.

Fiorella Nash, *The Abolition of Woman: How Radical Feminism Is Betraying Women.* San Francisco: Ignatius Press, 2018.

Abigail Shrier, *Irreversible Damage: The Transgender Craze Seducing Our Daughters.* Washington, DC: Regnery Publishing, 2020.

Wendy Shalit, *A Return to Modesty: Discovering the Lost Virtue.* New York: Free Press, 1999.

Edith Stein, *Essays on Woman.* Washington, DC: ICS Publications, 1996.

Alice Von Hildebrand, *The Privilege of Being a Woman*. San Francisco: Ignatius Press, 2005.

Matt Walsh, *What Is a Woman: One Man's Journey to Answer the Question of a Generation*. Nashville, TN: DW Books, 2022.

Chapter 3: Revisiting "Happily Ever After"

For Discussion

How is the Christian view of "happily ever after" different from the version we see depicted in popular culture and the media?

Why is it essential that marriage be the foundation of the family?

What are some ways that children benefit from being raised by a mother and a father?

How can the image of the Trinity be made manifest in "broken" or nontraditional families?

Co-parenting matching apps claim to reduce the "messiness" of the traditional family. What do they mean by this? What are some ways in which this practice creates its own "messes"?

Digging Deeper

BOOKS

Mary Eberstadt, *Primal Screams: How the Sexual Revolution Created Identity Politics.* West Conshohocken, PA: Templeton Press, 2019.

Kimberly Hahn, *Beloved and Blessed: Biblical Wisdom for Family Life.* Cincinnati: Servant, 2010.

Pope St. John Paul II, *Familiaris Consortio.* Washington, DC: USCCB Publishing, 1982.

Pope St. John Paul II, *Letter to Families.* Bedford, NH: Sophia Institute Press, 2015.

Pope St. John Paul II, *Mulieris Dignitatem.* Washington, DC: United States Catholic Conference, 1988.

Christopher and Jennifer Kaczor, *The Seven Big Myths about Marriage: What Science, Faith, and Philosophy Teach Us about Love and Happiness.* San Francisco: Ignatius Press, 2014.

VIDEO

Christopher Kaczor, "How Children Help Their Parents Flourish." Ted[X] Talk at Loyola Marymount, 2014.

Chapter 4: Contraception Versus a Culture of Hospitality

For Discussion

What is the contraceptive mentality, and where do you

see it at work in our world?

In what ways does contraception contribute to a less hospitable society?

How is contraception harmful to women's health? In what ways has contraception acted against women's advancement in society?

Why is it problematic to think of access to contraception as a basic right?

How does contraceptive mentality lead to widespread reliance on abortion?

Digging Deeper

BOOKS

Ryan T. Anderson and Alexandra DeSanctis, *Tearing Us Apart: How Abortion Harms Everything and Solves Nothing.* Washington, DC: Regnery Publishing, 2022.

Mary Eberstadt, *Adam and Eve After the Pill: Paradoxes of the Sexual Revolution.* San Francisco: Ignatius Press, 2013.

Jennifer Fulwiler, *Something Other than God: How I Passionately Sought Happiness and Accidentally Found It.* San Francisco: Ignatius Press, 2016.

Sarah E. Hill, Ph.D., *This Is Your Brain on Birth Control: The Surprising Science of Women, Hormones, and the*

Law of Unintended Consequences. New York: Avery Press, 2019.

Christopher Kaczor, *The Ethics of Abortion: Women's Rights, Human Life, and the Question of Justice*. Oxfordshire, England, UK: Routledge, 2010.

Pope St. Paul VI, *Humanae Vitae*. San Francisco: Ignatius Press, 2002.

Janet E. Smith, *Why Humanae Vitae Is Still Right*. San Francisco: Ignatius Press, 2018

VIDEOS

Dr. Janet Smith, "Contraception: Why Not." janetsmith.org, 2005.

Punam Kumar Gill, "Hush: A Liberating Conversation about Abortion and Women's Health." Mighty Motion Pictures, 2016.

WEBSITE

NaturalWomanhood.org (While this site is not Catholic, it promotes natural alternatives for women's health that can be very useful for Catholic women.)

Chapter 5: Unconditional Love Begins in the Womb

For Discussion

What are some ways in which prenatal testing might be licitly used?

Why might Catholic couples consider using prenatal testing?

What is the relationship between prenatal testing, abortion, and eugenics?

What are the limitations of this technology, and what problem does this pose?

Why might couples choose to forgo prenatal testing? Can you name reasons both practical and spiritual?

Digging Deeper

BOOKS
Emily di Ardo, *Living Memento Mori: My Journey Through the Stations of the Cross.* Notre Dame, IN: Ave Maria Press, 2020.
Barbara Katz Rothman, *The Tentative Pregnancy: How Amniocentesis Changes the Experience of Motherhood.* New York: W. W. Norton & Company, 1993.
Simone Troisi and Cristiana Paccini, *Chiara Corbella Petrillo: A Witness to Joy.* Bedford, NH: Sophia Institute Press, 2015.
Ted Peter, *For the Love of Children: Genetic Technology and the Future of the Family.* Louisville, KY: Westminster John Knox Press, 1996.

234 *Guides for Discussion and Digging Deeper*

VIDEO
"99 Balloons." Igniter Media, 2007.

ARTICLE
Dr. Christopher Kaczor, "Do Women Regret Giving Birth
    When the Baby is Doomed to Die?" *Public Discourse*,
    January 23, 2019.

WEBSITE
Be Not Afraid, benotafraid.net, a nonprofit supporting
    families experiencing a prenatal diagnosis and carry-
    ing to term.

PODCASTS
Samantha Stephenson, *Brave New Us*, episode 5: "Re-
    imagining the Role of Disability in God's Kingdom."
Samantha Stephenson, *Brave New Us*, episode 6: "What
    Makes a Life Valuable."

Chapter 6: This Is My Body, Given Up for You: Childbirth and the Paschal Mystery

For Discussion

How has power in the birthing process shifted away from
women over time?

What are some of the reasons to consider natural labor
and birth?

How are women's choices in birth limited by existing structures?

Why is it important for a woman to have a say in how she gives birth?

How can women connect childbirth with the Paschal Mystery? With Mary?

Digging Deeper

Books

Christy Angelle Bauman, *Theology of the Womb: Knowing God through the Body of a Woman*. Eugene, OR: Cascade Books, 2019.

Ina May Gaskin, *Ina May's Guide to Childbirth*. New York: Bantam Books, 2003.

Mary Haseltine, *Made for This: The Catholic Mom's Guide to Birth*. Huntington, IN: Our Sunday Visitor, 2018.

Milli Hill, *Give Birth Like a Feminist*. New York: HQ Publishing, 2019.

Leah Jacobson, *Wholistic Feminism: Healing the Identity Crisis Caused by the Women's Movement*. Ironton, MN: Lumen Press, 2021.

Rachel Jones, *A Brief Theology of Periods (Yes, Really)*. Epsom, England, UK: The Good Book Company, 2021.

VIDEO
Abby Epstein, *The Business of Being Born.* Netflix, 2008.

Chapter 7: My Flesh Is True Food: The Spiritual and Physical Nourishment of Nursing

For Discussion

What are some of the benefits of breastfeeding?

What are some of the challenges women face with breast-feeding in the United States?
What are some ways we might address these challenges at the individual, familial, community, workplace, and governmental levels?

Is it appropriate to classify breastfeeding as a social justice issue? Why or why not?

What is the connection between nursing and the Eucharist?

Digging Deeper

BOOKS
Laura Kelly Fanucci, *Everyday Sacrament: The Messy Grace of Parenting.* Collegeville, MN: Liturgical Press, 2014.

Sheila Kippley, *Breastfeeding and Catholic Motherhood:
    God's Plan for You and Your Baby*. Bedford, NH:
    Sophia Institute Press, 2005.

La Leche League, *The Womanly Art of Breastfeeding*. New
    York: Random House Publishing, 2010.

Ginny Moyer, *Random MOMents of Grace:
    Experiencing God in the Adventures of Motherhood*.
    Chicago: Loyola Press, 2013.

VIDEO

"Pope Speaks Out on Breastfeeding in Church." CBS, 2018.

Chapter 8: The Working Mom Dilemma

For Discussion

Why are phrases like "working mom" and "just a mom"
misleading?

Why has prioritizing motherhood become a countercul-
tural value? Why is it necessary?

What are some of the "shoulds" that you encounter surrounding the vocation of motherhood?

What are some of the ways you find balance in your
motherhood?

How is being open to discernment distinct from a permissive and relativistic view on family structures?

Digging Deeper

BOOKS

Mary Eberstadt, *Home-Alone America: The Hidden Toll of Day Care, Behavioral Drugs, and Other Parent Substitutes.* New York: Sentinel, 2004.

Kimberly Hahn, *Beloved and Blessed: Biblical Wisdom for Family Life.* Cincinnati: Servant, 2010.

Kimberly Hahn, *Graced and Gifted: Biblical Wisdom for the Homemaker's Heart.* Cincinnati: Servant, 2008.

Erica Komisar, LCSW, *Being There: Why Prioritizing Motherhood in the First Three Years Matters.* New York: TarcherPerigee, 2017.

Holly Pierlot, *A Mother's Rule of Life: How to Bring Order to Your Home and Peace to Your Soul.* Bedford, NH: Sophia Institute Press, 2004.

Dr. Laura Schlessinger, *In Praise of Stay-at-Home Moms.* New York: HarperLuxe, 2009.

Hubert Van Zeller, *Holiness for Housewives and Other Working Women.* Bedford, NH: Sophia Institute Press, 1997.

Chapter 9: Responding Faithfully to the Cross of Infertility (and Why That Doesn't Include IVF)

For Discussion

What are the options for couples facing infertility?

How does infertility connect us to women in Christian history?

How does IVF harm women? Marriage?

What are some ways that women have seen God work through their struggles with infertility?

How can we embrace our spiritual motherhood to accompany one another in suffering?

Digging Deeper

Catholic women sharing their infertility stories on Instagram: @emilystimpsonchapman, @findingphilothea, @catholicwifecatholiclife.

BOOKS
Colleen Carroll Campbell, *My Sisters the Saints: A Spiritual Memoir*. New York: Random House Publishing, 2012.

Janet Smith and Christopher Kaczor, *Life Issues, Medical Choices: Questions and Answers for Catholics.* Cincinnati, OH: Servant, 2010.

Carmen Santamaria and Angelique Ruhi-Lopez, *The Infertility Companion for Catholics: Spiritual and Practical Support for Couples.* Notre Dame, IN: Ave Maria Press, 2012.

PODCAST

Catholic Feminist, "In Vitro Fertilization and Pro-life OBGYN Work ft. Monique Ruberu."

Chapter 10: The Dark Realities of Gamete Donation and Surrogacy

For Discussion

Why are egg "donation" and surrogacy issues of social justice?

How do these practices commodify women and children?

Do we have a right to become parents? How does our answer to this question change our views of these practices?

What might the widespread practice of egg "donation" and surrogacy do to our understanding of motherhood?

How is surrogacy like adoption? How is it different? Why

does the Catholic Church permit adoption and prohibit surrogacy?

Digging Deeper

BOOKS

Dr. Charles C. Camosy, *Resisting Throwaway Culture: How a Consistent Ethic of Life Can Unite a Fractured People*. New York: New City Press, 2019.

Renate Klein, *Surrogacy: A Human Rights Violation*. North Melbourne, Australia: Spinifex Press, 2017.

Fiorella Nash, *The Abolition of Woman: How Radical Feminism Is Betraying Women*. San Francisco: Ignatius Press, 2018.

Amy Westervelt, *Forget "Having It All": How America Messed Up Motherhood — And How to Fix It*. New York: Seal Press, 2018.

VIDEOS

Lucie Jourdan, *Our Father*. Blumhouse Productions, 2022.

Jennifer Lahl, *Breeders: A Subclass of Women?*. The Center for Bioethics and Culture, 2014.

Jennifer Lahl, *Eggsploitation*. The Center for Bioethics and Culture, 2011.

PODCAST

Venus Rising.

Chapter 11: Brave New World

For Discussion

One of the objections to these technologies is that we are "playing God." Does this objection hold up? What is the problem with "playing God," and can we articulate it for nonbelievers?

How ought society deliberate on and regulate the research being done on these types of "treatments"?

How might "treatments" like this change the way we define family and even humanity itself?

How do we articulate the grave violations of dignity at stake with a generation that no longer holds anything as sacred?

Why would God allow us the power to create life if He didn't want us to use it? Doesn't He cooperate in the creation of every human person? Does that mean that God cooperates with evil?

Digging Deeper

BOOKS
Fr. Greg Boyle, *Tattoos on the Heart*. New York: Free
    Press, 2011.

Shannon Evans, *Embracing Weakness: The Unlikely
    Secret to Changing the World.* Huntington, IN: Our
    Sunday Visitor, 2019.

Aldous Huxley, *Brave New World.* New York: Harper
    Perennial, 2006.

Dr. Christopher Kaczor, *Disputes in Bioethics: Abortion,
    Euthanasia, and Other Controversies.* Notre Dame,

IN: University of Notre Dame Press, 2020.

C. S. Lewis, *The Abolition of Man.* New York: Harper
    One, 2015.

PODCAST
Samantha Stephenson, *Brave New Us* podcast, season 1,
    "Genetic Editing"

Chapter 12: Spiritual Motherhood: A Prophetic Calling

For Discussion

When is moral judgment appropriate and necessary?

What did Jesus mean when he said, "Judge not lest you be judged" (Mt 7:1)?

How is the cancel culture actually a culture of judgment?

Why is it our responsibility to proclaim the truth, even when that truth is difficult and messy?

What are some ways to witness to the truth *in love*?

Digging Deeper

BOOKS

Kimberly Cook, *Motherhood Redeemed: How Radical Feminism Betrayed Maternal Love.* Charlotte, NC: TAN Books, 2020.

John and Stasi Eldridge, *Captivating: Unveiling the Mystery of a Woman's Soul,* Nashville, TN: Thomas Nelson, 2011.

Gertrud von le Fort, *The Eternal Woman: The Timeless Meaning of the Feminine.* San Francisco, Ignatius Press, 2010.

ARTICLE

Jessica Ptomey, "The Mother in Every Woman" at Catholicmom.com

VIDEOS

Bishop Robert Barron, "Catholics, Media Mobs, and the Culture of Contempt." YouTube, 2021.

Sr. Miriam James Heidland. "Receiving the Gift of Femininity," GIVEN Institute, 2021.

For more information and resources, subscribe to Samantha Stephenson's *Brave New Us: Faith and Bioethics* newsletter at www.faithandbioethics.com.

Notes

Introduction

1. Alice von Hildebrand, Commencement Address, Christendom College, May 16, 2015, Front Royal, VA, YouTube, 30:37, https://media.christendom.edu/2015/05/5153/.

2. Russell Chandler, "Vatican Condemns Human Artificial Reproduction," *Los Angeles Times*, March 10, 1987, https://www.latimes.com/archives/la-xpm-1987-03-10-mn-5921-story.html.

Chapter 1

1. *The Collected Works of Edith Stein*, ed. Lucy Gelber and Romaeus Leuven, 2nd ed., vol. 2, *Essays on Woman* (Washington, D.C.: ICS Publications, 2017), 119.

2. G. K. Chesterton, *What's Wrong with the World* (San Francisco: Ignatius Press, 1994), 48.

3. Augustine of Hippo, *Confessions,* trans. Henry Chadwick (Oxford: Oxford University Press, 1998), 1.

Chapter 2

1. Pope Francis, interview by Antonio Spadaro, August 19, 2013, vatican.va.

2. Second Vatican Council, *Gaudium et Spes*, December 7, 1965, par. 24, vatican.va.

3. Leah A. Jacobson, *Wholistic Feminism: Healing the Identity Crisis Caused by the Women's Movement* (Ironton: Lumen Press, 2021), 48, emphasis added.

4. "Statistics and Research on Eating Disorders," *National Eating Disorder Association*, https://www .nationaleatingdisorders.org/statistics-research -eating-disorders.

5. Sophia Davis, "Periods on Display" *The Lancet*398, No. 10306 (September 25, 2021): 1124–1125. https://doi. org/10.1016/S0140-6736(21)01962-0; "Pregnant and Recently Pregnant People," CDC, March 3, 2022. https://www.cdc .gov/coronavirus/2019-ncov/need-extra-precautions /pregnant-people.html.

6. Grace Emily Stark, "Are You a Woman? Or a 'Body with a Vagina'?" *Verily*, October 1, 2021. https://verilymag .com/2021/10/news-the-lancet-bodies-with-vaginas -women-language-sex-differences-2021.

7. Ryan Glasspiegel, "UPenn Transgender Swimmer Lia Thomas Sparks Outrage by Shattering Women's Records," *NY Post*, December 2, 2021. https://nypost.com/2021/12/02/ upenn-transgender-swimmer-sparks-outrage-by -shattering-womens-records/.

8. Jesús Manuel García-Acosta et al., "Trans* Pregnancy and Lactation: A Literature Review from a Nursing Perspective," *International Journal of Environmental Research and Public Health*17 (1), no. 44 (19 December 2019). https://doi. org/10.3390/ijerph17010044,

9. Michael Cook, "Male Mice Give Birth in Bizarre Chinese Experiment," *BioEdge,* July 17, 2021. https://bioedge.org/uncategorized/male-mice-give-birth-in-bizarre-chinese-experiment/.

10. Christopher and Jennifer Kaczor, "The Fourth Big Myth: Cohabitation Is Just Like Marriage," in *The Seven Big Myths about Marriage: What Science, Faith, and Philosophy Teach Us about Love and Happiness* (San Francisco: Ignatius Press, 2014), 104.

11. Congregation for the Doctrine of the Faith, *Donum Vitae*, February 22, 1987, II. A par. 3, vatican.va.

Chapter 3

1. John Paul II, *Familiaris Consortio*, November 22, 1981, no. 12.

2. Ibid., no. 14.

3. Ibid., no. 20.

4. Ibid., no. 43.

5. "Modamily reimagines relationships" is what the website says of itself on its homepage, Modamily.com.

6. Branwen Jeffries, "Do Children in Two-Parent Families Do Better?" *BBC News*, February 5, 2019, https://www.bbc.com/news/education-47057787.

7. John Paul II, "Homily," Holy Mass at the Capitol Mall in Washington, DC, October 7, 1979, par. 5, vatican.va.

Chapter 4

1. Chiara and Enrico Petrillo, "Letter to Francesco," trans. Tatum. Quoted in Lisa Cotter, "Saints Are Still Being Made," Focus, January 10, 2013, https://focusequip.org/saints-are-still-being-made-meet-chiara-corbella-petrillo/.

2. Christopher and Jennifer Kaczor, "The Fifth Big

Myth: Premarital Sex Is No Big Deal," in *The Seven Big Myths about Marriage*, 139.

3. Grace Emily Stark, "The Violence of Birth Control," *Mere Orthodoxy*, prepublication.

4. Ibid.

5. John Paul II, *Evangelium Vitae*, March 25, 1995, par. 13, vatican.va.

6. Ellen Wiebe et al., "Reasons for Requesting Medical Assistance in Dying," *Canadian Family Physician/Medecin de famille canadien*, 64, no. 9 (September 2018): 678. https://www.cfp.ca/content/cfp/64/9/674.full.pdf.

7. Bradford Richardson, "Insurance Companies Denied Treatment to Patients, Offered to Pay for Assisted Suicide, Doctor Claims," *Washington Times*, May 31, 2017. https://www.washingtontimes.com/news/2017/may/31/insurance-companies-denied-treatment-to-patients-o/.

8. "U.S. Contraceptive Market Size, Share & Trends Analysis Report By Product (Pills, Condoms, Vaginal Ring, Subdermal Implants, IUD, Injectable), And Segment Forecasts, 2020–2027," Grand View Research, https://www.grandviewresearch.com/industry-analysis /us-contraceptive-market.

9. Gerard Migeon, "CDC Changes Effectiveness Rating on Fertility Awareness Methods," Natural Womanhood, May 27, 2019. https://naturalwomanhood.org/cdc-changes-effectiveness-rating-on-fertility-awareness-methods-2019/.

10. Gerard Migeon, "Is Natural Family Planning Good for Marriages, and Do Fertility Apps Have the Same Potential?" *Public Discourse*, August 19, 2021. https://www.thepublicdiscourse.com/2021/08/77264/.

11. John Paul II, *Familiaris Consortio*, no. 32.

12. Ibid.

13. Jean M. Twenge, *iGen: Why Today's Super-Connected Kids Are Growing Up Less Rebellious, More Tolerant, Less Happy—and Completely Unprepared for Adulthood—and What That Means for the Rest of Us* (New York: Atria Books, 2017), 22.

Chapter 5

1. Barbara Katz Rothman, *The Tentative Pregnancy: How Amniocentesis Changes the Experience of Motherhood* (New York: Viking Penguin, 1986), 35.

2. Ibid., 23.

3. *Donum Vitae*, I, 2.

4. Ibid. Italics in original.

5. Ted Peters, *For the Love of Children: Genetic Technology and the Future of the Family.* (Louisville, KY: Westminster John Knox Press, 1996), 90.

6. Bridget Mora, "Prenatal Testing and the Denial of Care," *Ethics & Medics* 43, no. 2 (February 2018):1–4.

7. Interview with Bridget Mora, *Brave New Us* podcast.

8. Ibid.

9. Ibid.

10. Madeline P. Nugent, *My Child, My Gift: A Positive Response to Serious Prenatal Diagnosis* (Hyde Park, NY: New City Press, 2008), 15.

11. Sarah Zhang, "The Last Children of Down Syndrome," *The Atlantic*, December 2020, https://www.theatlantic.com/magazine/archive/2020/12/the-last-children-of-down-syndrome/616928/.

12. Ibid.

13. Rothman, 35.

14. "Prenatal Tests Have High Failure Rate, Triggering Abortions," NBCNews, December 14, 2014, https://www.nbcnews.com/health/womens-health

/prenatal-tests-have-high-failure-rate-triggering
-abortions-n267301.

15. American College of Obstetricians and Gynecologists, "Committee Opinion No. 640: Cell-Free DNA
Screening for Fetal Aneuploidy," *Obstetrics and Gynecology* 126, no. 3 (September 2015): e31–e37. DOI: 10.1097/
AOG.0000000000001051.

16. Denis Cavanaugh et al., "Changing Attitudes of
American OB/Gyns on Legal Abortion," *The Female Patient*
20 (May 1995).

17. Robert Meyer et al, "Survival of Children with
Trisomy 13 and Trisomy 18: A Multi-State Population-Based
Study," *American Journal of Medical Genetics* 170, no. 4 (April
2016): 825–837, https://www.ncbi.nlm.nih.gov/pmc/articles
/PMC4898882/pdf/nihms787880.pdf.

18. Michelle d'Almeida et al., "Perinatal Hospice: Fam-
ily-Centered Care of the Fetus with a Lethal Condition,"
Journal of American Physicians and Surgeons 11, no. 2 (Summer 2006): 55. https://www.jpands.org/vol11no2/calhoun.
pdf; Byron Calhoun et al., "Perinatal Hospice. Comprehen-
sive Care for the Family of the Fetus with a Lethal Condition," *Journal of Reproductive Medicine*, 48, no. 5 (May 2003):
343–348.

19. Christopher Kaczor, "Do Women Regret Giving
Birth When the Baby Is Doomed to Die?" *Public Discourse*,
January 23, 2019, https://www.thepublicdiscourse
.com/2019/01/47802/.

20. Heidi Cope, "Pregnancy Continuation and Organi-
zational Religious Activity Following Prenatal Diagnosis of
a Lethal Fetal Defect Are Associated with Improved Psychological Outcome," *Prenatal Diagnosis* 35, no. 8 (August 2015):
761–768.

Chapter 6

1. Alison Young, "Deadly Deliveries: A USA Today Investigation," *USA Today,* March 22, 2021, https://www.usatoday.com/story/news/investigations /2021/03/22 /deadly-deliveries-usa-today-investigation /4802861001/.

2. Milli Hill, *Give Birth Like a Feminist: Your Body. Your Baby. Your Choices* (London: Harper Collins, 2019), 23.

3. Jacobson, *Wholistic Feminism*, 56.

4. Hill, *Give Birth Like a Feminist*, 129–130.

5. Jacobson, *Wholistic Feminism*, 55.

6. "Preliminary Statistics," *The Farm Midwifery Center*, thefarmmidwives.org/preliminary-statistics.

7. Jessi Klein, "Get the Epidural," *New York Times,* July 9, 2016, https://www.nytimes.com/2016/07/10/opinion /sunday/get-the-epidural.html.

8. Abby Epstein, *The Business of Being Born* (Burbank, CA: New Line Home Entertainment, 2008).

9. Hill, *Give Birth Like a Feminist*, 173.

10. Epstein and, *The Business of Being Born*.

11. "Maternal Mortality and Maternity Care in the United States Compared to 10 Other Developed Countries," The Commonwealth Fund Issue Briefs, November 18, 2020, https://www.commonwealthfund.org/publications /issue-briefs/2020/nov/maternal-mortality -maternity-care-us-compared-10-countries.

12. Epstein, *The Business of Being Born*.

13. Hill, *Give Birth Like a Feminist*, 26.

14. CDC, "Racial and Ethnic Disparities Continue in Pregnancy-Related Deaths," US Department of Health and Human Services press release, September 6, 2019, https://www.cdc.gov/media/releases/2019/p0905-racial-ethnic -disparities-pregnancy-deaths.html.

15 Epstein, *The Business of Being Born*.

16. Hill, *Give Birth Like a Feminist*, 122–123.

17. Ina May Gaskin, *Ina May's Guide to Childbirth* (New York: Random House, 2003) 189.

18. Kimberly Hahn, *Beloved and Blessed: Biblical Wisdom for Family Life* (Steubenville: Emmaus Road Publishing, 2021).

19. John Paul II, "Letter to Families," 1994, par. 11, vatican.va.

20. Tim Staples, "Was Mary Free From Labor Pain?" *Catholic Answers*, September 6, 2021, https://www.catholic.com/magazine/online-edition/was-mary-free-from-labor-pain.

21. Gaskin, *Ina May's Guide to Childbirth*, 153–160.

22. Grantly Dick-Read, *Childbirth Without Fear: The Principles and Practices of Natural Childbirth* (London: Heinman, 1968).

23. Hill, *Give Birth Like a Feminist*, 144.

24. J. Sandall et. al., "Midwife-led Continuity Models Versus Other Models of Care for Childbearing Women," Cochrane Database of Systematic Reviews, Issue 4 Art. No.: CD004667 (2016). doi: 10.1002/14651858.CD004667.pub5.

Chapter 7

1. Grace Emily Stark, "Catholic Social Teaching and America's Suboptimal Breastfeeding Rate: Where Faith and Policy Should Meet to Combat Injustice," *The Linacre Quarterly* 84, no. 4 (2017): 357. https://doi.org/10.1080/00243639.2017.1384268.

2. Pamela Morrison, "How Often Does Breastfeeding Really Fail?" La Leche League International, November 12,

2018, https://www.llli.org/how-often -does-breastfeeding -really-fail/.

3. Ibid.

4. World Health Organization, *Acceptable Medical Reasons for Use of Breast-Milk Substitutes* (Geneva: WHO Press, 2009), 8–9.

5. "The Baby Friendly Hospital Initiative," Baby Friendly USA, https://www.babyfriendlyusa.org/about.

6. Arthur I. Eidelman, et al., "Breastfeeding and the Use of Human Milk," *Pediatrics* 129, no. 3 (March 2012): 827–841. https://doi.org/10.1542/peds.2011-3552.

7. Stark, "Catholic Social Teaching and America's Suboptimal Breastfeeding Rate," 358.

8. Ibid.

9. Ibid.

10. E. Jensen, "Participation in the Supplemental Nutrition Program for Women, Infants and Children (WIC) and Breastfeeding: National, Regional, and State Level Analyses," *Maternal & Child Health Journal*, 16: 624–31. DOI: 10.1007 /s10995-011-0796-7.

11. Ibid.

12. Stark, "Catholic Social Teaching and America's Suboptimal Breastfeeding Rate," 357.

13. Jensen. "Participation in the Supplemental Nutrition Program for (WIC) and Breastfeeding," 625.

14. U.S. Department of Labor, Fair Labor Standards Act: Section 7 (r). 29 U.S.C. 207 (Washington D.C.: 2010), https:// www.dol.gov/agencies/whd/nursing-mothers/law.

15. John Chrysostom, *Baptismal Catechesis* 3.17–19, in *Liturgy of the Hours,* Good Friday, Office of Readings, 2nd Reading.

16. Caroline Walker Bynu, *Holy Feast and Holy Fast: The*

Religious Significance of Food to Medieval Women (University of California Press: Los Angeles, 1987), 263–268.

17. Ibid., 270-271.

18. Julian of Norwich, *Revelations of Divine Love* (1901), ch. 59–60, https://earlybritishlit.pressbooks.com/chapter /julian-of-norwich-revelations-of-divine-love-selections/.

19. Danielle Rose, "A Mother's Communion," *Culture of Life* album, 2015. Used with permission.

20. Laura Kelly Fanucci, *Everyday Sacrament: The Messy Grace of Parenting* (Collegeville, MN: Liturgical Press, 2014), 52–54.

21. Ginny Kubitz Moyer, *Random MOMents of Grace: Experiencing God in the Adventures of Motherhood* (Chicago: Loyola Press, 2013), 82.

Chapter 8

1. D'Vera Cohn, Gretchen Livingston, and Wendy Wang, "After Decades of Decline, a Rise in Stay-at-Home Mothers," Pew Research Center, April 8, 2014, https://www. pewresearch.org/social -trends/2014/04/08/after-decades-of-decline-a-rise-in-stay-at-home-mothers/.

2. Pope Francis, interview by Antonio Spadaro, August 19, 2013, vatican.va.

3. John Paul II, "Letter to Women," June 29, 1995, par. 2, vatican.va.

4. This section is adapted from a portion of Samantha Stephenson, "Dismantling the 'Just a Mom' Myth," *FemCatholic*, December 5, 2019, https://www.femcatholic.com/post /dismantling-the-just-a-mom-myth.

5. Kelley Dawson, "A Mother for All Seasons," *FemCatholic*, November 2, 2017, https://www.femcatholic.com /post/a-mother-for-all-seasons.

6. Erica Komisar, *Being There: Why Prioritizing Motherhood in the First Three Years Matters,* (Penguin Random House: New York, 2017), 40–41.

7. Ibid., 37.

8. Ibid., 41.

9. Ibid., 42.

10. Louis J. Puhl, trans. *The Spiritual Exercises of St. Ignatius,* (Chicago: Loyola Press, 1951), 4.

11. John Paul II, *Mulieris Dignitatem,* August 15, 1988, par. 31, vatican.va.

12. Haley Stewart, "Don't Let Strangers on the Internet Tell You What's Best for Your Family," *Carrots for Michaelmas,* https://www.carrotsformichaelmas.com/2019/08/25/dont-let-strangers-on-the-internet-tell-you-whats-best-for-your-family/.

Chapter 9

1. *Catechism of the Catholic Church,* 2nd ed. (Washington DC: United States Catholic Conference, 2011), no. 2360.

2. John Paul II, *Familiaris Consortio,* par. 11.

3. *Donum Vitae,* II.B, par. 4, emphasis added.

4. Cassandra Stone, "Gabrielle Union Shares Grief over Choosing Surrogacy," *Motherly,* September 13, 2021, https://www.mother.ly/life/news/celebrity-news/gabrielle-union-surrogate-struggles.

5. Kaczor and Kaczor, *The Seven Big Myths about Marriage,* 206.

6. Jacobson, *Wholistic Feminism,* 50.

7. Ibid.

8. Kaczor and Kaczor, *The Seven Big Myths about Marriage,* 206.

9. "Biotechnology and Public Policy: Biotechnologies

Touching the Beginnings of Human Life," President's Council for Bioethics, sec, 3.4, January 2004, https://bioethicsarchive.georgetown.edu/pcbe/background/bppinterim.html.

10. Congregation for the Doctrine of the Faith, *Dignitas Personae*, September 8, 2008, vatican.va. Original emphasis retained.

Chapter 10

1. *Donum Vitae*, II.A par. 3, and sec. III.

2. Fiorella Nash, *The Abolition of Woman: How Radical Feminism Is Betraying Women* (San Francisco: Ignatius Press, 2018), 87.

3. Jonathan Edwards, "Families Say a Fertility Doctor Used His Own Sperm to Impregnate Patients. Now, He Must Pay Them Millions," *Washington Post*, July 30, 2021, https://www.washingtonpost.com/nation/2021/07/30/fertility-doctor-wrong-sperm/.

4. "Ovarian Hyperstimulation Syndrome," *Cleveland Clinic*, 2021, https://my.clevelandclinic.org/health/diseases/17972-ovarian-hyperstimulation-syndrome-ohss.

5. Stark, "The Violence of Birth Control," *Mere Orthodoxy*, prepublication.

6. Tasha McAbee, "Egg Donation Risk and Reward," *Public Health Post*, October 9, 2020, 2022, https://www.publichealthpost.org/viewpoints/egg-donation-risk-and-reward.

7. Sandra G. Boodman, "Do Women Who Donate Their Eggs Run a Health Risk?" *Washington Post*, June 20, 2016, https://www.washingtonpost.com/national/health-science/do-women-who-donate-their-eggs-run-a-health-risk/2016/06/20/8755b22e-1c7a-11e6-b6e0-c53b7ef63b45_story.html.

8. Jane Brody, "Do Egg Donors Face Long-Term Risks?"

New York Times, July 10, 2017, https://www.nytimes
.com/2017/07/10/well/live/are-there-long-term-risks-to-egg
-donors.html.

9. "Egg Donation Risks: What are the Side Effects of
Becoming an Egg Donor?" Bright Expectations Southern
California Reproductive Center, December 11, 2017, https://
www.brightexpectationsagency.com/blog/egg-donation
-risks/.

10. Melinda Guy, "Pros and Cons of Egg Donation,"
Family Tree Surrogacy Center, https://familytreesurrogacy
.com/blog/pros-cons-egg-donation/.

11. "Risks of Egg Donation," Happy Beginnings, LLC,
https://www.happybeginningseggdonation.com/donor/risks
-of-egg-donation/.

12. "How Many Eggs Do I Donate?" Bright Expectations
Southern California Reproductive Center, August 9, 2018,
https://www.brightexpectationsagency.com/blog/how-many
-eggs-do-i-donate/. I was unable to verify these claims with
ASRM, and the link provided by the clinic on its website was
unrelated. Bright Expectations let my requests for the source
of their claim go unanswered.

13. "Future Fertility: If I Donate My Eggs, Can I Still
Have Kids?" Bright Expectations Southern California Reproductive Center, February 1 2018, https://www
.brightexpectationsagency.com/blog/fertility-after-egg
-donation/.

14. Zohreh Shahhosseini, et al., "A Review of the Effects
of Anxiety during Pregnancy on Children's Health," *Maternal
Sociomed* 27, no. 3 (June 2015): 200–202, https://www.ncbi
.nlm.nih.gov/pmc/articles/PMC4499279/.

15. Jennifer Lahl and Matthew Eppinette, *Breeders: A
Subclass of Women?* (San Ramon, CA: Center for Bioethics

and Culture, 2014).

16. Katherine Drabiak, "Infants Born Through Surrogacy Contracts Cannot Be Canceled or Returned," *Harvard Law Bill of Health*, February 8, 2021, https://blog.petrieflom.law. harvard.edu/2021/02/08/surrogacy-contracts-canceled/.

17. "Three Things You Should Know about Surrogacy," Center for Bioethics and Culture, https://cbc-network.org/ wp-content/uploads/2022/02/3_Things_You_Should _Know_About_Surrogacy-Center_for_Bioethics_and _Culture.pdf.

18. Grace Emily Stark, "Renting Wombs, Rending Hearts: The Dark Realities of Surrogacy," *Verily,* January 26, 2021, https://verilymag.com/2021/01/surrogacy-altruistic -commercial-exploitation-women-children-2021.

19. Justo Aznar and Miriam Martínez Peris, "Gestational Surrogacy: Current View," *Linacre Quarterly* 86, no. 1 (2019): 57. doi: 10.1177/0024363919830840.

20. Nirmala George, "India's Lucrative Surrogacy Business Has Been Shut Down," *Star Tribune*, December 24, 2015, https://www.startribune.com/india-s-lucrative-surrogacy -business-has-been-shut-down/363333171/.

21. *Wombs for Rent: Surrogate Motherhood in India*, RT Documentary, https://rtd.rt.com/films/wombs-for -rentindia-surrogacy-for-pofit/.

22. Gena Corea, "What the King Can Not See" in *Embryos, Ethics and Women's Rights,* ed. Elaine Hoffman Baruch, Amadeo F. D'Adamo, Jr. and Joni Seager (Haworth Press: New York, 1988).

23. "Facts & Stats," Home for Every Child Adoption Society, https://www.homeforeverychild.org/facts-and-stats.

24. Mike Feibus, "CRISPR Gene Editing Tool: Are We Ready to Play God?" *USA Today*, July 24, 2017, https://www

.usatoday.com/story/tech/columnist/2017/07/24/crispr
-gene-editing-tool-we-ready-play-god/490144001/.

Chapter 11

1. C. S. Lewis, *The Abolition of Man* (New York: Harper Collins, 2001), 59.

2. Samantha Stephenson, "Huxley's Brave New World Is Here," *Crisis Magazine*, February 21, 2022, https://www.crisismagazine.com/2022/huxleys-brave-new-world-is-here. Quoting John Paul II, *Angelus*, November 30, 1986, par. 3, vatican.va.

3. Lewis, *Abolition of Man*, 55.

4. John Conley, "Margaret Sanger's Extreme Brand of Eugenics," *America*, July 28, 2020, https://www.americamagazine.org/politics-society/2020/07/28/margaret-sangers-extreme-brand-eugenics.

5. "Juvenile Death With Dignity? UK Case May Hurt Aid in Dying Push," *NBC News*, November 4, 2014, https://www.nbcnews.com/health/health-news/juvenile-death-dignity-u-k-case-may-hurt-aid-dying-n242961.

6. "Netherlands Backs Euthanasia for Terminally Ill Children Under-12," *BBC News*, October 14, 2020, https://www.bbc.com/news/world-europe-54538288.

7. Alberto Guiblini and Francesca Minerva, "After-Birth Abortion: Why Should the Baby Live?" *Journal of Medical Ethics*, vol. 39 (2013): 261. http://dx.doi.org/10.1136/medethics-2011-100411.

8. David Cyranoski, "The CRISPR-Baby Scandal: What's Next for Human Gene Editing?" *Nature*, February 26, 2019, https://www.nature.com/articles/d41586-019-00673-1.

9. Lewis, *Abolition of Man*, 57.

10. Simon Usborne, "I Thought — Who Will Remember

Me? The Man Who Fathered 200 Children," *The Guardian*, November 24, 2018, https://www.theguardian.com /science/2018/nov/24/sperm-donor-man-who-fathered-200 -children.

11. Sarah Zhang, "The Children of Sperm Donors Want to Change the Rules of Conception," *The Atlantic*, October 15, 2021, https://www.theatlantic.com/science/archive/2021 /10/do-we-have-right-know-our-biological-parents/620405/.

12. Elizabeth Armstrong Moore, "'Genius' Sperm Bank Donor, Who's Schizophrenic, Turns Self In," *USA Today*, September 3, 2016, https://www.usatoday.com/story/news /nation-now/2016/09/03/genius-sperm-donor-whos -schizophrenic-turns-self/89825220/.

13. "Artificial Womb Keeps Premature Lambs Alive for Weeks. Are Humans Next?" *PBS News Hour*, April 26, 2017, https://www.pbs.org/newshour/health/artificial-womb -keeps-premature-lambs-alive-weeks-humans-next.

14. Christopher Kaczor, "Could Artificial Wombs End the Abortion Debate?" *National Catholic Bioethics Quarterly* 5(2): (Summer 2005): 283–301.

15. Stephenson, "Huxley's Brave New World Is Here," *Crisis.*

16. Daniel Goleman, "The Experience of Touch: Research Points to a Critical Role," *New York Times*, February 2, 1988.

17. Eino Partanen, et al., "Learning-Induced Neural Plasticity of Speech Processing Before Birth," *Proceedings of the National Academy of Sciences* 110, no. 37 (September 10, 2013):15145–15150. https://doi.org/10.1073/pnas .1302159110.

18. Phillip Ball, "Reproduction Revolution: How Our Skin Cells Might Be Turned into Sperm and Eggs," *Guardian*,

October 14, 2018, https://www.theguardian.com /science/2018/oct/14/scientists-create-sperm-eggs -using-skin-cells-fertility-ethical-questions.

19. Saskia Hendricks, et al., "Artificial Gametes: A Systematic Review of Biological Progress Towards Clinical Application," *Human Reproduction Update*21, no. 3, (May/June 2015): 285-296. https://doi.org /10.1093/humupd/dmv001.

20. Jessica Hamzelou, "World's First Baby Born with New '3 Parent' Technique," *New Scientist,* September 27, 2016, https://www.newscientist.com/article/2107219 -exclusive-worlds-first-baby-born-with-new-3-parent -technique/.

21. Henry T. Greely, "Human Reproductive Cloning: The Curious Incident of the Dog in the Night-Time," *Stat,* February 21, 2020, https://www.statnews.com/2020/02/21 /human-reproductive-cloning-curious-incident-of-the-dog -in-the-night-time/.

22. Gregory Boyle, *Tattoos on the Heart: The Power of Boundless Compassion* (New York: Free Press, 2010), 190.

23. William Wordsworth, "The Virgin," https://www .poetryfoundation.org/poems/45563/the-virgin.

Chapter 12

1. Zenit, "Alice von Hildebrandt on Feminism and Femininity," EWTN, November 26, 2003, https://www.ewtn.com /catholicism/library/alice-von-hildebrandt-on-feminism -and-femininity-2764.

2. John XXIII, *Mater et Magistra,* May 15, 1961, vatican .va.

3. John Paul II, *Familiaris Consortio,* no. 33.

4. Julie Otsuka, *Buddha in the Attic* (Random House: New York, 2011), 10.

5. "6 September (1955): Flannery O'Connor to Betty Hester," *The American Reader*, https://theamericanreader .com/6-september-1955-flannery-oconnor/.

About the Author

SAMANTHA N. STEPHENSON is a Catholic wife, home-schooling mama of four, and host of the *Brave New Us* podcast. She holds master's degrees in theology and bio-ethics, and her writing has been featured at Blessed Is She, Catholic Mom, *Crisis* Magazine, *The Federalist*, FemCath-olic, Natural Womanhood, Notre Dame's Grotto Net-work, *Our Sunday Visitor*, and *Verily* Magazine. Follow her blog at MamaPrays.com or sign up for her newsletter at FaithandBioethics.com to receive the latest updates on medical research, technology, and culture.